# THE NOSTALGIA OF STEAM

42394

# THE NOSTALGIA OF STEAM

## Journeys round Britain

**Edited by Mike Esau**

Silver Link Publishing Ltd

First published in 1994
Reprinted 2001

British Library Cataloguing in Publication Data

A catalogue record for this book is available from the British Library

ISBN 1 85794 166 7

Silver Link Publishing Ltd
The Trundle
Ringstead Road
Great Addington
Kettering
Northants
NN14 4BW

Tel/Fax: 01536 330588
email: sales@nostalgiacollection.com
Website: www.nostalgiacollection.com

Printed and bound in Great Britain

The number appended to each caption is the negative number. Requests for prints may be made via the Publishers.

***Half title*** **Kelso, Borders; BR '2MT' 2-6-0 No 78049, 12.07 pm Kelso-St Boswells, 20 July 1963.**
A sunny Saturday afternoon. I'm on my way from Berwick, where I'm staying with a friend above his large grocery shop and there's a scent of tobacco in my bedroom from the storehouse below, to Shank End and Whitrope on the Waverley route. The engine and one composite coach of 1st and 2nd Class accommodation shuttled up and down to St Boswells and made a twice-weekday sortie to Berwick-on-Tweed still recalling the division of the line between the North British and North Eastern Railways prior to the 1920s. The service was withdrawn in 1964. *2936*

***Page 2*** **Penybont Junction, Powys; LMS '4MT' No 42394, 7.45 am Swansea (Victoria)-Shrewsbury, 19 August 1959.**
I'm driving from Newbridge-on-Wye to Tregaron in order to photograph the eastern end of the Central Wales and the northern portion of the Mid-Wales lines and to be ready for the Carmarthen-Aberystwyth route next day. Unusually I'm at track level with the kind agreement of the signalman in the box behind me. I say more above this picture on page 50. *1778*

***Title page*** **Llanwrda, Dyfed; GWR '56XX' 0-6-2T No 5656, ECS from Llangadog-Llandovery school train, 30 May 1962.**
Trains run each day mainly for school children used to be quite rare, and as public timetables failed to supply details of school holidays it was unwise to include them in itineraries. Today County Councils are obliged by law to convey children to school, so contracts for trains are not unknown. The 4.05 pm from Whitby, for instance, contains an extra unit exclusively for the children. This picture shows the empty stock returning at 4.18 pm to Llandovery. *2656*

***Opposite page***
Where the first journey began. Fareham Station on 16 October 1954, with the 6.48 pm to Alton via the Meon Valley standing in the bay with LSWR 'M7' 0-4-4T No 30054 at its head. *490*

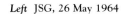

***Left*** **JSG, 26 May 1964**
I had plenty of time to set up my equipment prior to the passage of the Stranraer-Dumfries train over the viaduct. The problem was how to link the Ferrograph with my photographic position high on the hillside nearby (see page 8). In the event I decided not to use it, but not before testing its frequency response from the car battery with a tape of 'My Fair Lady', the strains of which disturbed and sounded quite out of place in these bleak surroundings. *Alan Lillywhite*

***Below*** **JSG 1993.**
At work on the book. *Gavin Mist*

# Contents

**Marton Junction, Warks; LMS '2MT' 2-6-2T No 41323, 4.55 pm Napton & Stockton-Leamington Spa (Milverton), 21 June 1958.**
Just see how straight the line was to Rugby from Leamington Spa, yet like so many other cross-country routes in the Midlands, BR failed to capitalise on them and ran tired three-coach sets behind Class '5' locomotives dawdling from one local station to the next on 19th-century schedules. Trains even called at some villages on market days that had long become irrelevant. The services should have been speeded up. Peterborough, for instance, a New Town, was connected with expanding towns such as Wellingborough and Northampton, and to need to close such a link through lack of traffic when the numbers of cars and lorries on the equivalent roads are seen today, is little short of culpable neglect of a national asset! One wonders what the role of the then Ministry of Transport was in all this waste. *1333*

# Introduction

This book illustrates journeys round Britain in the mid-1950s and early '60s when steam trains were commonplace and before The Rt Hon Ernest Marples, as Minister of Transport, began implementing the recommendations of Dr Beeching for line and station closures.

In practical terms the journey began at Fareham Station in Hampshire on 16 October 1954 when Hugh Davies, then Secretary of the Railway Enthusiasts' Club, Farnborough, Hampshire, introduced me to Harry Grenside whilst waiting for the 6.48 pm to Alton via the Meon Valley to get going; he was an elderly gentleman who owned a factory making valve-guides for motor cycles. We thought what a pleasant way this was to explore the countryside in a relaxed fashion and, after meeting Alan Lillywhite, an employee of Lloyds Bank of my own age, on Ian Allan's 'The Lickey Limited' on 16 April 1955, the three of us set about methodically covering the whole network of BR using service trains with circular tour tickets, special trains, and, where the passenger service had been withdrawn, goods trains (with brake-van permits as illustrated below).

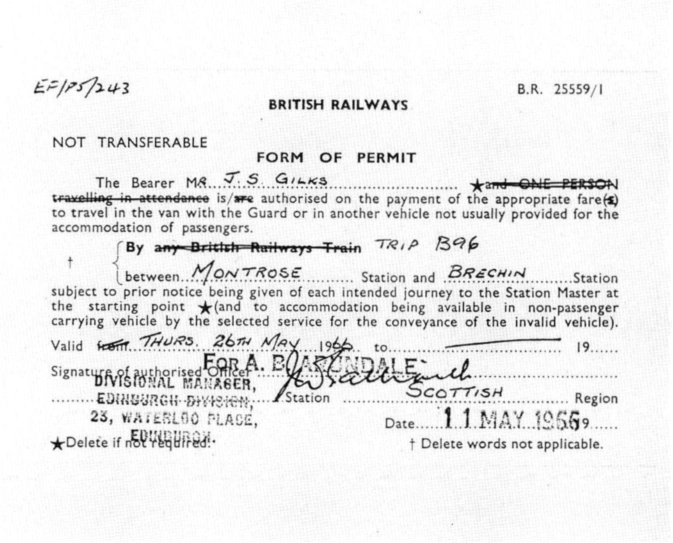
EF/175/243

B.R. 25559/1

**BRITISH RAILWAYS**

NOT TRANSFERABLE

**FORM OF PERMIT**

The Bearer MR J. S. GILKS ★~~and ONE PERSON travelling in attendance~~ is/~~are~~ authorised on the payment of the appropriate fare(~~s~~) to travel in the van with the Guard or in another vehicle not usually provided for the accommodation of passengers.

† By ~~any British Railways Train~~ TRIP B96
between MONTROSE Station and BRECHIN Station

subject to prior notice being given of each intended journey to the Station Master at the starting point ★(and to accommodation being available in non-passenger carrying vehicle by the selected service for the conveyance of the invalid vehicle).

Valid ~~from~~ THURS. 26TH MAY 1966 to ———— 19.....

Signature of authorised Officer FOR A. B. ARUNDALE

DIVISIONAL MANAGER, EDINBURGH DIVISION, 23, WATERLOO PLACE, EDINBURGH. Station SCOTTISH Region

Date 11 MAY 1966

★Delete if not required. † Delete words not applicable.

By the end of 1959 we 'three men in a train' had already made 37 organised trips of our own. I used to look out of the carriage window for vantage points for photography and then travel back in the car to augment the pictures we had taken. It is a selection of these photos that you are about to see, not in date or geographical order according to our tour, but under a series of headings, with happenings on our journey providing some of the continuity.

I owe the idea of the book to Mike Esau who has been badgering me politely for years to get on with it. He printed some of the negatives long ago in the hope that I would make a move. But it has taken the interest of Silver Link Publishing and the example of their fine 'Classic Steam' series finally to make me give it priority. Mike has now put it together. I hope you enjoy it as much as I have enjoyed helping to assemble the pictures and reminiscing about them.

My intention is to produce a book that will appeal to all those with an interest in railways - who are nostalgic for journeys past; who, as parents or grandparents, want to provide a lasting memento for their families who have experienced steam on preserved lines or special trains; who are fascinated by stations and lines long gone, both locally and nationally; or who are just enthusiasts.

When the railway was being built from London to Southampton in 1838 the townsfolk of Kingston upon Thames, where I was born, objected to it (just like protesters do to proposed motorways today) and it was obliged to run through a hill at a place that became known as Surbiton. A deep cutting had to be dug and this intersected a cart-track for which the railway company had to provide a bridge over the line. Because it was unimportant the parapets were not of masonry but of an open lattice structure through which a small boy in his push-chair could see the trains passing below. The bridge, now carrying King Charles's Road, shook me as the steam expresses rushed beneath, leaving behind that unique aroma of smoke and hot oil which I have always relished. The eyes, ears and nose were all affected by the experience.

My interest in railways remained largely dormant until shortly before National Service in 1951, and really came to life on 30 April 1952. I was attending a course in Manchester, and for some reason breakfast was delayed that day so I wandered out to a book shop and bought *The Railway Magazine* for the first time. Returning to the restaurant I happened to sit opposite Hugh Davies, a total stranger to me, and he enquired whether I was interested in trains. I must have answered 'Yes' because we travelled home to London together, not direct to Euston but on the 12.35 pm from London Road to Leicester Central, which, because it was Friday, called at Crowden and Woodhead, so I had the experience of entering the single-bore tunnel at the latter place in steam days from a standing start. I thought we were never coming out! Later the train took the loop line from Staveley Central to Springwood Tunnel in order to call at Chesterfield Central. We duly arrived in Leicester at 4.27 pm (nearly four hours after leaving Manchester). The 4.45 pm express reached Marylebone at 7.10 pm.

In retrospect I realise that I enjoyed the unusual experience at Woodhead, the amble round the coalfields through scenery of a kind I had not seen before, and that I acquired a new interest in the mode of travel apart from the journey itself. What would the engine be? Which company had built the rolling-stock? Why did the line take the course it did through the countryside? Why did it pass over a trunk route at Rugby without any physical connection? I have never been a trainspotter. Recording the number of the engine is a chore associated with photography rather than amusement. But I have always looked out of the window with map in hand.

The other item to hand would be the timetable. I love timetables! For years when the new BR issue arrived I looked first to see if the 17.42 from Paddington to Birmingham (New Street) had survived as the only passenger train regularly to travel via Greenford. This year (1993) its equivalent is the 09.20 to Aylesbury via High Wycombe. It must run to keep drivers familiar with the route and to avoid the closure procedure. Then how many trains serve Reddish South and Denton? The current answer is one each week in one direction only, calling on Fridays at 14.01 and 14.05 respectively. Will there be more than one passenger train each week direct from Carnforth to Morecambe? Did you know that it's advisable to allow ten minutes between connections from the former Great Northern to the former Great Central Railways at Retford because of the walk along the platform?

And this fascination is greater when the Working Timetable and Special Traffic Notice, for staff use, is added. These show that trains from Maesteg to Cardiff, for instance, use the Leckwith spur in the up direction so as to call at the former Barry line platforms; and that to provide the rolling-stock for a charter from Cleethorpes to Portsmouth Harbour the empty coaches were scheduled to pass through Crowle at 15.15 the previous afternoon.

This information is of great value, if not essential, when photography is involved. Coupled with the 1-inch or equivalent Ordnance Survey map, and Mike Esau's Sun Spot Chart (ever hopeful!), a car-based itinerary can be planned using minor roads and entailing visits to communities you would never otherwise see. The final ingredient for a happy and contented day out is *The Good Food Guide*, so that one's successes (and failures) can be discussed over dinner.

The importance of photography was brought home to me when, in April 1955, my first serious article about railways was published in *Railway World*. I needed illustrations and acquired an Ensign Selfix camera for the purpose. My neighbour at that time was Cine-Manager at Wallace Heaton in Bond Street, London, when it was still an independent firm, and he advised on the camera to buy, which he said would bring out detail in the shadows under station awnings when used with Kodak Panatomic-X film.

This was for the black and white pictures that you will see in this book. (The number under each one equates with the negative in the collection.) When I began regular lectures at evening classes I needed colour slides which I took and which are now available in limited numbers from Colour-Rail (Chesham, Bucks) and Pictorail (Lyth, Kendal, Cumbria), and are included, with prints from the black and white negatives of the John Gilks Collection, in videos produced by Gavin Mist Video Services (Nawton, North Yorkshire). All the pictures in the body of this book have been taken by me. For this purpose I purchased first an Agfa Silette and later a Leica M4 and a Rolleiflex 3.5f.

'Talking of Trains', my evening class at Surbiton, began on 27 September 1960 with the title 'The Development of Railways in Surrey', and continues to this day under the stewardship of Dr Gerald Siviour, whilst I moved north permanently in 1983 and began 'Talking of Trains (North)' at Malton. The large numbers attending my classes were not welcomed by the HQ of the Workers Educational Association, but naturally the far-sighted unprejudiced local WEA appreciated the financial results. Among the 70 people who were eventually on the register at Surbiton (now over 80!) most of the professions were represented and I was fortunate with the advice and facilities freely available to me, even including the removal of furniture from the south to my present home in the north. And then in the autumn of 1976 a new student joined - Gavin Mist - who soon became and has remained my best and most trusted friend.

The slides are backed up by original tape recordings made at the lineside from April 1961 when I purchased a Ferrograph tape recorder and converter to run it from a car battery (see page 4). Hardly to the very high standard set by Peter Handford every time, but on much the same basis; he kindly gave me advice. I have since read that he suffered much the same problems in the early days but had the patience to persist. He was even prepared to go out at night. He concentrated on recording sound, which was his profession, and developed Transacord. I decided to emphasise photography, one of my hobbies. For a while I was operating recording gear and at the same time a black and white camera on a tripod with a long remote control cable to a bulb under my foot, and holding a colour camera to my eye. Ridiculous! Something had to give, and it was the sound recording.

Both the sound and visual recordings have survived to achieve archive status. This aspect of the hobby was enhanced when in 1983 I was invited to become Secretary of the Friends of the National Railway Museum, and was asked to record features of the railway scene that were likely to disappear. The General Manager of the then Eastern Region of BR, Frank Paterson, and his PROs were particularly helpful in this and invited me to attend lunch in the Officers' Mess as a guest from time to time to be updated on possible changes ahead. Track permits were provided and complimentary 1st Class tickets when appropriate. I also had the good fortune to become more acquainted at this time with Dr John Coiley who was Keeper of the NRM.

Turning to my professional career in local government, this really blossomed when I joined one of the Local Authority Associations in London in 1968 to advise on town planning and transport matters at policy level. These Associations, when they join together, are very powerful political organisations to whom governments listen and who listen carefully to governments. With reorganisation in 1974 my post grew in importance (and the tourism brief was soon added) and we absorbed another association connected with municipal buses. This provided me with the opportunity to run, in effect, two national transport conferences each year, and I soon brought the railways into their ambit.

By chance, the organiser of my WEA class at Surbiton was mother of the Chief Commercial Officer of BR at the time - Peter Keen - so we had already met socially at his instigation. I now invited the Board Member, Marketing, of BR - Bob Reid (later to become the first Chairman of that name) - to give a paper, which he gladly did, much to my delight. Over lunch afterwards he expressed a wish for officers of BR and the LAAs to become more acquainted so that problems on both sides could be explored and tackled in a frank and positive way. Regular quarterly meetings were the result. I like to think that real progress was made; certainly stations began to reopen and new ones to be built, partnership schemes developed with mutually sensible financial arrangements and some stability resulted. This could not have been achieved, of course, without party political consensus.

Naturally this high-level involvement with BR overflowed into my hobby, though I was always at pains to keep my professional railway interest and my enthusiasm apart. Indeed, to such an extent that many did not know of my railway hobby. I have since learned, however, that several top-ranking officials of BR were apprehensive at meetings about my detailed knowledge of the network compared to their own!

One of the happiest consequences of this personal close co-operation with BR was the opportunity to charter saloons normally privy to the General Manager (these were diesel-operated and so do not appear in this book). This came about at the instigation of the Chief Passenger Manager of the Eastern Region, Bert Gemmell, who was aware of the evening class, knew how disciplined were its members and thought that they would appreciate the privilege. We did! From July 1974 we used first the Wickham Saloon, then the Stourton Saloon and finally, as part of the activities of the Friends of the NRM, the Engineer's Saloon at York until each DMU was condemned (not through our doing!). When Bert moved to Scotland as Director of Public Affairs he arranged for a loco to be coupled to two saloons and ultimately also a kitchen and dining car. We had really marvellous trips to our own itineraries which I shall never forget. Sadly, when he retired we were (deliberately?) priced out of the market. But the sequel to retirement was the creation of 'The Sidings' restaurant near York which has become much more than just a consolation prize. The 'Talking of Trains (North)' group hold their annual buffet there and we often arrange events to take advantage of the fine cuisine and the unique railway environment.

Being outside the industry, naturally I was regarded initially with some suspicion by the transport men. I have always felt that my three-year stint on the Council of the Chartered Institute of Transport was my least constructive. (They had previously refused membership for 14 years as I did not quite fit!) The priorities of those around me seemed quite foreign and I could not contribute. Representatives of the various modes seemed intent on putting their corner first and co-ordination was a coincidental by-product. This world is, of course, a politician's dream, and my colleagues seemed to me to be unaware that at a stroke these same politicians could upset their datum lines if they didn't pull together. In my experience so many transport people have been taken aback at the word 'politics' - we don't want to be involved in that! Hence the transport problems since the war. One of the main beacons of hope at that time was, to my mind, the Director-General of the CIT, Brigadier Donald Locke, whose friendship I have come greatly to value (and that of his wife, Joan). He has helped me reach the pinnacle of my career by inviting me (through Bob Davies, former DG of West Yorkshire PTE) to join the transport livery company, the Worshipful Company of Carmen, and to become a Freeman of the City of London.

I need to get down now to some nitty gritty matters about the book. Indeed, it could be regarded as a book within a book, for the narrative text is stimulated by the pictures but embraces more than might appear at first sight.

The caption to each picture begins with its location (using station names from 1955 and local government areas as in April 1974), then details of the locomotive and its train, and the date on which it was taken; finally there is more detail of the scene and the circumstances in which it was recorded. Obviously a good pre-Grouping railway gazetteer and Ordnance Survey map could enhance enjoyment of the book and help to find the precise whereabouts of the picture, if desired.

In conclusion may I thank most sincerely Will Adams, Editor of Silver Link Publishing Ltd, for giving me the opportunity to present the book, Mike Esau for his expertise and tenacity, John Edgington for his research and detailed knowledge of railways past and present, Ian Cantlon for scrutinising the photo captions, and last but by no means least, Gavin Mist for his encouragement and patience. I hope it has all been worthwhile and that you will like it too!

***Right***
This picture is described in the narrative (page 180). I can be seen slightly right of centre, waving and wearing an RAF beret, retained from National Service days, in order to keep the smuts from the engine out of my hair. To my left and slightly taller, wearing a cap, is Harry Grenside, and to my right, also wearing a cap, is Alan Lillywhite. Next but one to his right is Gerald Daniels, the well-known organiser of steam trains in the south whilst with BR. John Edgington has a mop of dark hair in the foreground. The photograph was taken as the train entered the Benwick goods branch at Three Horse Shoes.

# 1. Waiting for the train

Train journeys, more than any by car, coach or plane, create in me a spirit of apprehension, and more today than ever before. This could be a sign of age, but I think it is a growing lack of confidence in a revenue-starved organisation, and this I regret. I sense, however, that I am not alone in this when waiting at the station.

The people in the pictures that follow may be experiencing similar anticipation; an adventure is about to begin, there is an air of uncertainty; something novel is bound to take place.

Have I got my ticket? Will the train be on time and will it get there on time and maintain connections? Why doesn't the announcer mention *my* train? Will my reserved seat be there? How will I move an awkward intruder? Will the seat face the engine? Will it really be non-smoking? Will the train be warm? Will it be cold? What will the nearby passengers be like - will there be some lunatic extrovert with a mobile phone or parents whose children control them rather than the right way round? Will the dining-car be manned? What's for dinner?

These feelings must stem from the fact that someone else is in charge; the faceless ones in Control, for instance. There is little we can do about dissatisfaction in the short term.

My apprehension must hark back to childhood. As a toddler I'm told that I screamed every time I was taken on a train. It's family folklore that, in readiness for a journey to the West Country, my father took me frequently from Norbiton, our local station, to the next one at New Malden and back. (What consideration my parents showed for other passengers!) The experience must have had the desired effect for on the night of the journey from Paddington to St Austell I slept soundly all the way!

Just think how much of my life has been spent waiting for trains; on the platform itself - though mercifully not that much, as most trains run to time despite what the media might lead us to believe - and at the lineside , where the longest stint was 3¾ hours near Frome hanging about for a 'Blue Peter' special to come by.

Naturally I have sought to avoid predictable delays such as missing the last train from Cheltenham when *en route* from Newbury to Andover (14 June 1958). This had the habit of leaving Savernake Low Level so promptly that it passed the westbound local between there and Wolfhall Junction unless a letter was sent to the Station Master (see above right).

1, Norbury Villas,
Hawks Road,
Kingston-upon-Thames,
Surrey.

11th June, 1958.

Dear Sir,

On Saturday next, 14th June, I shall be arriving at Savernake (Low Level) Station with two other friends on the train from Newbury which arrives at 7.41 p.m.

We are anxious to catch the 7.44 p.m. to Andover, and in view of the tight connection I should be obliged if you could assist us by taking any steps that may be within your power to ensure that these trains do in fact connect on Saturday, normal circumstances permitting.

Yours faithfully,

The Stationmaster,
Savernake (Low Level) Station,
Near Marlborough,
Wilts.

Even such a letter didn't have the desired effect on 18 May 1964. The departure of the freight from Ladybank to Perth was timed close to the arrival of the DMU from Dundee. As Alan and I alighted we could see a plume of smoke on the northern horizon. Embarrassment all round. Not to be outdone, however, the Station Master phoned Newburgh for the freight to be held there. He then commandeered a loco from the nearby yard and we chased the train, catching up with it in the loop some eight miles ahead. There we were brought alongside the brake-van and clambered across, much to the relief of the Polish guard. He had known we were due but the driver had known better!

Waiting for trains at Three Cocks Junction (page 163) proved memorable. In the refreshment room on 5 May 1958 I was asked whether I preferred whole cream or half-cream in my coffee; on 30 May 1962 I was requested by a sweep to tell him when his brush had emerged from the top of the waiting-room chimney!

With other passengers, I had unusual waits for trains on the Worcester line on 6 May 1955 and 17 July 1979 respectively. The late morning service from Oxford then ran through to Chipping Norton. Customers, however, had to alight at Kingham - whatever the weather - cross the footbridge and wait at the branch platform for the GWR railcar to catch them up. This was for safety reasons associated with a crossover on the main line which presumably had no facing point locks. At Moreton in Marsh trains in opposite directions terminated simultaneously in the early evening. Apparently identical units, they, and their crews, were nevertheless allocated to different depots and could not proceed further. So through passengers had to get out and wait whilst the trains swapped over!

People waiting at the triangular junction station at Shipley have to be prepared to move quickly to whichever platform is served by the first train to Keighley or Bradford. Further north, at Giggleswick, they are provided with a set of wooden steps to gain access to the train from platforms that have to be brought up to conventional height even yet!

Waiting for the Malton train at the new Manchester Airport station, my friend David Humphreys observed from the TV screen that it had been cancelled. On contacting an Inspector he was told that it was held at Piccadilly and could be brought along if he wished. He did - and it was!

Not everyone enjoys waiting at a station. The late Professor Joad described Reading on a wartime BBC *Brains Trust* programme as 'dull, ugly, noisy, gloomy, rather smelly, frightfully insalubrious and at all seasons of the year having an east wind blowing grit into your eyes'. His time there was 'punctuated by occasional visits to those places that gentlemen do visit when they're waiting for trains'.

The customers waiting at Newport, Salop, in 1962 (below) should have been advised by the porter, who in turn should have heard from the nearby signalman, if their train was delayed. This still happens at my local station, Malton (though only before lunchtime, when the staff go home), and is much appreciated. Unstaffed stations cannot represent BR in the business and social life of the community - the railway industry becomes marginalised; there is no one to attend Rotary or Round Table; and if someone comes from HQ he is bound to be regarded with suspicion.

The signalman/porter at Bow Brickhill (below), where in 1957 the platforms were even lower than Giggleswick actually helped young mothers lift their children and prams into the train despite being crippled himself.

**Newport, Shropshire; LMS '4MT' 2-6-4T No 42186, 12.20 pm Shrewsbury-Stafford, 27 October 1962.**
An everyday scene at the time. Saturday afternoon and people, wrapped up against the autumn chill, are bound for Stafford to do their shopping - few supermarkets in those days! It was still possible to carry most provisions in a couple of carrier bags. The station signs are more than 40 years old, having been erected by the London & North Western Railway. A horsebox connects the locomotive to the ex-LMS coaches. The tank on the left supplies the water columns at the platform ends to replenish loco boilers when necessary. The third lady from the right is conscious of my camera and is giving me a smile - at least I assume that's the reason! The line - from Wellington to Stafford - was unusual in being built by a canal company, the Shropshire Union. *2768*

**Bow Brickhill Halt, Bucks; LMS '2MT' 2-6-2T No 41329, 12.45 pm Bedford (St John's)-Bletchley, 19 September 1957.**
A Thursday this time. I had picked up Alan at Esher, taken pictures at Cowley, near Uxbridge, Chesham, Tring and Swanbourne and arrived here around lunchtime. Do notice the old-fashioned prams the kindly porter/signalman will be handling. There are collapsible steps on the rear coach for access; the next is a double-ended Brake 3rd of LNWR origin and could have been a slipcoach (see text on page 36); the nearest is an LMS 3rd Open converted to a driving trailer for pull-and-push working. The waiting shelter is a standard LNWR prefabricated building. *1097*

**Witham, Essex; LNER 'B1' 4-6-0 No 61280, express from London (Liverpool Street), and GER 'J19/2' 0-6-0 No 64656, RCTS special from Dunmow, 10 August 1958.**
I'm on board the train this time - the RCTS Special on the far side of the picture. We have travelled via Dunmow and will now reverse to go eventually through Halstead to Cambridge where a third reversal will take us to Bedford and Harpenden. There a second train, with fewer coaches, will take us to Hemel Hempstead and back. I can still recall the mad rush over the footbridge there to gain one of the smaller number of seats. I wonder whether footbridges are ever checked in anticipation of a crowd? The planks of the bridge at Appleby were elevated once by the steam pressure of Duchess of Hamilton on a run-past. *1390*

**Windermere, Cumbria; LMS '4MT' 2-6-4T No 42317, 2.50 pm from Oxenholme, 24 May 1959.**
It is the detail of the station that fascinates me. Do notice that the clock is by a local clockmaker - W. Hill of Lancaster - rather than the ubiquitous 'Joyce - Whitchurch'. Wyman's bookstall, before being taken over by John Menzies, carries a poster about Donald Campbell's latest exploits with his speedboat on Lake Coniston. The long short trousers worn by the boy are now in vogue again.

The whole atmosphere is one of bustle and purpose, but subsequently the station went very down market, although it has bobbed up again as a Tourist Information Centre. It is a pity that the engineers were so ruthless in removing all but one track at the time of post-Beeching rationalisation so it is difficult to run other than multiple unit trains to this potentially popular destination. Hitherto there were regular through services during the summer months from such obvious holiday resorts as Blackpool, providing an afternoon excursion. *1628*

**Portsoy, Grampian; BR '4MT' 2-6-0 No 76108, 6.30 pm Aberdeen-Elgin, 2 June 1959.**
Until recently this picture was the one I had taken latest on any given day, being at about 8.40 pm. Now it has been superseded by the 'Orient Express' north of Hartlepool at 8.45 pm (3 July 1993)!

I'm surprised so many people are about to travel towards Elgin where we are to stay overnight. The previous night had been spent at Kintore so that we could travel to Alford and back on the goods. This was so timed that we were likely to miss our train north to the Buchan coast unless we reached Inverurie earlier. Hence we arranged for the goods to call at Kemnay where, in the grass-grown station approach, waited Mr W. J. Wallace with his new Rover 100 taxi. For a fee of 10 shillings he cut the corner off the railway and set us down for the train to Tillynaught and Banff and then to Portsoy where we took dinner, as we would be too late for this at our overnight hotel. *1694*

**Newton Stewart, Dumfries & Galloway; LMS '4MT' 2-6-4T No 42689, 8.05 am Stranraer (Town)-Dumfries, 22 July 1963.**
Whilst at Berwick on Tweed (see page 4) I made an excursion to Galloway and spent a Sunday night in Newton Stewart. The following morning I took this picture of people setting off for Dumfries. In the background are the junction signals for the line down the Isle of Whithorn (illustrated on page 117). On the platform is a barrow-load of mail, and a Post Office van is waiting on the down side for the letters from London. The train is composed of ex-LMS stock. *2948*

**Verwood, Dorset; BR '4MT' 2-6-0 No 76016, 10.04 am Bournemouth (West)-Salisbury, 21 May 1963.**

A Tuesday, and my diary is silent except for the initials 'HCLG' meaning that Harry was involved. There are very few passengers (though a lady is powdering her nose), but plenty of freight in the yard, including five ferry vans (which could be SNCF?). Do notice that the platforms are lit by oil lamps (1963!). *2884*

**Chandlers Ford, Hants; LSWR 'M7' 0-4-4T No 30130, 2.20 pm Romsey-Eastleigh, 7 September 1957.**

I like this picture very much. On the right another lady is engaged in her toilette before joining the train - I wonder what would be said if a man shaved on the platform? The train is made up of London & South Western stock at least 40 years old, with the guard's lookout very conspicuous. The station signs date from the Southern Railway era. I believe that this was the last day on which steam-hauled local services ran in the area, diesel multiple units being due to take over the following Monday. The station closed on 5 May 1969 and today a single track suffices for the irregular service this way. *1083*

**Ventnor, Isle of Wight; LSWR 'O2' 0-4-4T No 30 *Shorwell*, from Ryde (Pier Head), 19 April 1959.**
Two pictures illustrating what have since become vintage cars! At Ventnor there are coal cells in the cliff on the left, a Southern Railway sign which lasted until closure in 1966 (that must have paid for itself!) and there is a ship's gangway on the island platform which was used to enable passengers to reach the exit when both lines were occupied by trains at the height of the summer. The engine will take water from the adjacent column and run round its coaches for the return to Ryde Pier head. *1585*

**Clutton, Avon; GWR '57XX' 0-6-0PT No 9729, 4.05 pm Frome-Bristol (Temple Meads), passing BR '3MT' 2-6-2T No 82044, light engine, 16 May 1959.**
CJX 144 was owned by my friend Geoff Hunt and we travelled many happy miles together in it. On this occasion we concentrated on photographing the North Somerset Line from Bristol to Frome via Radstock, and I'm conscious that I am away from home on my widowed mother's birthday. There is a typical GWR cast iron nameboard on the signal box. *1613*

# 2. Station nameboards

The nameboard at Godwin's Halt is probably the one most memorable to me, and you could well ask why. You might even have difficulty in knowing the whereabouts of the place. It was situated on the branch from the Midland near Harpenden to Hemel Hempstead, which was closed to all traffic in 1964. It so happened that Hugh and I came across it during a photographic expedition by car on Sunday 7 March 1954. As passenger trains had ceased to call in 1947 it was no surprise to find the nameboard lying face-down on the grass-grown platform. What a pity it should go to waste - how could we acquire it legally for the REC Clubroom?

First it was necessary to be able to describe its position accurately. To attain this end we gently lifted it over the fence on to some adjoining Water Board land where it was more conspicuous but difficult for any individual to steal. Then Hugh wrote to the railway people. The sequel was a knock at the door of his home in Sycamore Road, Farnborough, when a huge parcel was delivered by road - with the compliments of the authorities! Presumably the freight train had made a special call at the halt; the guard, with the aid of the driver and fireman, had managed to retrieve the sign; and it had been taken to a siding near St Albans. Sent on from there to St Pancras, it would have gone across to Waterloo and down the Southern main line to the nearest parcels depot. What super service!

Beware of stations with nameboards such as 'Llanbister Road' (page 52) on the Central Wales Line. If you intend to alight there, make sure you know your next move. Great Western Railway timetables warned by footnote that the station was 5 miles from Llanbister; I recall others that said '$5\frac{3}{4}$ miles'. In any event what the timetable did not say was that the journey was by lonely minor roads up and down over several hills; also, which would have been more helpful, that by alighting two stations further west, namely at Penybont, there was a regular bus service to Llanbister. Perhaps that's why the current BR timetable makes no mention of the geographical situation. Why the same GWR timetable also pointed out with a footnote for Llandrindod Wells that it was $4\frac{1}{2}$ miles to Newbridge-on-Wye station I have never fathomed. Surely intending passengers would have travelled via Builth Road and changed trains there.

In a way there were two stations at Builth Road (page 40), a high and a low level, and we'll return to that later. Until 1975 there were also two stations in Gloucester. The GWR timetable used to state that there were 250 yards between its Central station in Gloucester and the Midland's Eastgate station. They were connected by a high enclosed footbridge.

On 21 May 1956 Harry, Alan and myself were travelling from Southampton by the Midland & South Western route to Ross-on-Wye and Symonds Yat. This meant joining the southbound 'Pines Express', a train renowned more for its fine appearance than its timekeeping, at Cheltenham Lansdown at 1.50 pm and then the 2.05 pm from Gloucester Central. This could be done, *but how* could it be guaranteed? I wrote to the Station Master at Gloucester Central explaining the position, and he replied that all would be well. Indeed it was! The 'Pines' was dead on time at Eastgate. We all made a dash for the stairs to the footbridge where a porter was standing to make sure we went the right way first time. From the top of the stairs the narrow corridor of the bridge looked endless, but we all ran the full length, 250 yards. Imagine our consternation when, on reaching the foot of the steps at Central, another porter told us that the train was in the bay platform at the far end and would we please hurry. We did and the guard opened a door for us into a corridor crammed with people intending to spend the Bank Holiday afternoon in the Wye Valley. The train steamed out immediately with us wedged in the throng.

'Journey Information' in the BR passenger timetable today gives recommended minimum times for changing between trains at certain stations. For instance, when arriving at York you should allow at least eight minutes if you hope to make a recognised connection. If you have to change stations, in Glasgow, for example, you should allow half-an-hour between arrival at Central and departure from Queen Street.

Additional nameboards at Appleford and Dilton Marsh Halts advised passengers to get their tickets from the Post Office, and from 'Mrs H. Roberts, "Holmedale", 7th house up the hill' respectively.

Two of the following pictures merit special mention (pages 22 and 23 respectively). The village of Ballingham in Hereford & Worcester is located on a peninsula in a bend of the River Wye, so is somewhat isolated from the road network. The railway crossed the river twice in this vicinity and so provided a well-sited station which was closed in 1964. The villagers became so cut off that the AA funded one of the first community buses, to ply to and from Ross-on-Wye, and I wrote an appraisal of it for *Drive* magazine.

Chedworth station closed three years earlier but had been served by only one train each way for some time and was unstaffed. This presented the local lengthman/platelayer with a problem. How did he get his wages? He collected them from the guard of the 2.33 pm every Saturday afternoon!

**Craven Arms & Stokesay, Shropshire; LMS Class '5' 4-6-0 No 45422, 3.00 pm Shrewsbury-Swansea (Victoria), 18 April 1960.**
**Knucklas Halt, Powys; LMS Class '5' 4-6-0 No 45298, 12 noon Shrewsbury-Swansea (Victoria), 19 August 1959.**
The westbound service over the Central Wales Line is in evidence here, and two totally different types of station nameboard, not to mention the award for the best maintained section of permanent way in the neighbourhood. The sign at Craven Arms is a fine GWR example and is fully comprehensive, including Brecon (involving a change of station and train at Builth Road), and Carmarthen, Tenby and Pembroke, reached via the branch from Llandilo. There is a bay out of the picture on the left from which some trains originated. BR totem signs hang from Great Western gas lamps, while Knucklas can only muster oil lighting. *1914/ 1781*

**Castle Ashby & Earls Barton, Northants; LMS Class '5' 4-6-0 No 45044, Northampton (Castle)-Peterborough (East).**
**LMS '2MT' 2-6-2T No 41227, Northampton (Castle)-Wellingborough (Midland Road), both 2 November 1963.**
The significance of these two almost identical pictures is the trains. They are included at this point because of the marvellous station name - Castle Ashby & Earl's Barton. The first train is of London & North Western (legally even of London & Birmingham!) Railway origin and will call here on its way from Northampton to Peterborough. The other, from Northampton to Wellingborough (Midland Road) only, is of Midland Railway origin and will not stop even though it's 40 years since the two companies were amalgamated as the LMS, whose style of nameboard is affixed to the signal box. There are oil lamps on both platforms. *3026/3027*

**Ketton & Collyweston, Leics; BR '4MT' 4-6-0 No 75059, Leicester/ Nottingham-Gorleston-on-Sea, 1 September 1962.**
**Yelvertoft & Stanford Park, Northants; LMS Class '5' 4-6-0 No 45324, 8.49 am Birmingham (New Street)-Peterborough (East), 26 October 1963.**
Two double-barrelled station names! I visited the first during a wonderful sunny day taking pictures in the Welland Valley, mainly of Summer Saturday extras to and from the Midlands and the East Coast. There is an Eastern Region blue enamel nameboard on display, a Midland Railway signal on the up line and that company's signal box peeping out from behind the building on the left. Both stations have adjacent level crossings.

The LMS 'Hawk's-eye' nameboard at Yelvertoft has been extended to cover the extra words and is possibly the longest of its type. Earlier I had called at Lilbourne, the next station to the west, which, until closure in 1966, stood adjacent to and almost beneath the M1 motorway at the point at which the M6 diverges. This junction necessitates a wide carriageway above the River Avon and the elderly porter at Lilbourne station confided in me that he had watched the pile-driving for the bridge with great interest. His father had told him that when the railway was being built the engineers had had great difficulty in finding firm ground for the permanent way. Now he observed the motorway engineers having the same problem. Millions of pounds might have been saved had they but consulted him first. And that's probably true! *2746/3024*

**Wakerley & Barrowden, Leics; LMS '4MT' 2-6-4T No 42061, 1.38 pm Rugby (Midland)-Ely, 7 November 1958.**
**Same location, LMS '6P/5F' 2-6-0 No 42955, eastbound freight, 1 September 1962.**
'Look what a year can bring' runs the old song, and these pictures show what can happen within four years. I can recall that the buildings on the down platform were held up by brick piers embedded in the meadow below and supported by the embankment on which the station stands. Presumably instability resulted and they had to be demolished. The LMS 'Hawk's-eye' nameboard with black letters on a yellow background (originally reflective glass beads, yellow) has survived to be painted in Eastern Region blue with white letters. Both sets of buildings, dating from LNWR days, look tatty in 1958. The main brick entrance building remains (since closure in 1966) as a private house. Presumably it still contains the fine wide stone staircase which led to the up platform. This station used to be east of Yelvertoft on the Seaton-Peterborough section of the same line. *1449/2749*

**Yatton, Avon; GWR '57XX' 0-6-0PT No 9601, freight from Cheddar, 10 October 1960.**
This time I'm taking the picture whilst changing trains. Alan Lillywhite and I are travelling from Paddington to Bristol, Severn Beach, Clevedon, Witham, Westbury and home via Salisbury where we had dinner at 'The Crown'. Another fine GWR nameboard tells us where to go. The centre-pivoted signals on the main line to Taunton facilitate sighting. There is a 'parachute' water tank for thirsty engines and elaborate barge-boards on the end of the signal box. *2258*

**Clarbeston Road, Dyfed; GWR '57XX' 0-6-0PT No 9760, 2.10 pm from Fishguard Harbour, 19 May 1961.**
I always feel far away from home when in West Wales (and in West Cumbria too) and can almost believe that I am already in Ireland. The station at Clarbeston Road survives and the junction for Fishguard, but the port no longer has a stopping service. Look at the proliferation of signals now replaced by one colour light! The nameboard is GWR blue enamel; a BR totem is fixed to the lamp-post. There are GWR four-wheeled platform barrows (with wheels smaller than those of other companies). I am changing trains with Harry and Alan; we are staying two nights in Carmarthen and the previous evening Harry's nephew had taken us out for a ride on a demonstration Dennis fire engine. *2418*

**Trefeinon, Powys; LMS '2MT' 2-6-0 No 46519, 9.55 am Moat Lane Junction-Brecon, 20 August 1959.**
**Ballingham, Hereford & Worcs; GWR 'Manor' 4-6-0 No 7801 *Anthony Manor*, 10.20 am Hereford-Gloucester (Central), 31 October 1964.**
Two stations with Great Western nameboards, the former on the Cambrian section. Here the signal box is switched out so that the signals remain clear in both directions over the up road.

The letters 'GWR' are entwined in the seat supports at Ballingham. This was the last day of the passenger service, and I wondered why over a line that, because of the many crossings of the Wye (which could have been costly in maintenance), provided a very direct route between two provincial cities. On winter Sundays, when the Severn Tunnel was in occupation by the engineers, the up and down Manchester/Liverpool-Plymouth expresses passed this way and were scheduled sometimes to cross at Fawley, the route being single track. That evening we recorded the last trains and the detonator explosions at Ross-on-Wye, but the tape recorder failed to operate consistently and the results were sub-standard. I'm told that with modern gear these recordings can be 'ironed out'. *1787/3340*

**Chedworth, Glos; SR 'U' 2-6-0 No 31795, 1.52 pm Cheltenham Spa (St James's)-Southampton (Terminus), 12 March 1960.**
As the Western Region had reduced the service between Southampton and Cheltenham via Marlborough and Cirencester to just one train each way and on weekdays only, I took every opportunity to photograph it in the glorious Cotswold scenery. Chedworth is a superb village and, in my view, the line did not intrude on the environment in any way. Do refer to the text about why the man is standing on the platform (page 16). The blue enamel signboard of the M&SWJR has survived from the opening day. There is another picture at Chedworth on page 134. *1888*

**Horspath Halt, Oxon; 4.45 pm Oxford-Princes Risborough, 27 March 1961.**
Normally I would never photograph the rear end of a train, but in this case it has succeeded. I wonder why? The nameboard and halt, of sleeper construction and probably only of one coach length (thus not now normally acceptable to the Health & Safety Executive), is pure Great Western. Ironic perhaps that the train is composed of ex-LMS stock. Funnily enough, I'm just returning from another visit to Chedworth! *2364*

# 3. Station architecture

The variation in appearance of station buildings is one of the many fascinations of railway travel, and I hope that the following small selection of photos does justice to the subject.

The High and Low Level station was one such characteristic. The Low Level at Builth Road is illustrated (page 40) as is that at Hengoed (page 97). In the first case the High Level has survived; in the latter it has been closed. One of the oddest, in my view, was called Hope. Situated amidst fields (and not to my recollection even in the parish of Hope) four miles east of Mold in Clwyd, it served the Ruthin-Chester line downstairs (where another station only half-a-mile east was called Hope & Penyffordd) and upstairs, trains between Wrexham and New Brighton (now Bidston only) or Chester (also calling only a quarter-mile south at Pen-y-ffordd (sic) station and two miles further on at Hope Village station). The 'double-deck' platforms stood at right-angles to each other. I alighted there from Ruthin (scheduled at 4.12 pm) with Alan Lillywhite on 13 May 1958 and climbed the stairs to board, at 4.36 pm, a train from Chester (Northgate) to Wrexham. The exchange station closed the following September and passenger trains from Ruthin ceased in 1962. The upper-deck service continues, non-stop, because Mrs Barbara Castle, when Minister of Transport, after ruminating for two years over her decision, did not adopt BR's recommendation for closure. It didn't stop her authorising the closure of 606 other route miles whilst in office, however.

Rolleston (page 26), at the junction of the Mansfield line with the Midland from Nottingham to Lincoln, serves Southwell Racecourse and thus has considerable significance to me. For it was an article I contributed to the REC magazine published in June 1954, about the importance of race traffic to railways throughout their history (and emphasising the role of the Southern Region), that led to my first meeting with BR management.

A letter dated 2 July 1954 arrived from the Public Relations Officer of the Western Region, one Cyril Rider. It read that he would 'be pleased to arrange for facilities, in particular, for Newbury race-course on this Region, if [I] would like to travel down and attend a meeting there'. The first I knew of the letter (which had been sent to the Clubroom) was when I read it in the July magazine. This was an object lesson to me; let no one believe that administration/communication is any worse today than it has ever been!

And so it was that on 13 August 1954 I found myself in a large room at Paddington, sitting before a large desk being addressed by rather a large, benign gentleman who treated me like a Dutch uncle. I shall never forget his kindness and the magic carpet I walked on with BR henceforth (until the 1990s perhaps when, temporarily, dead money assumed greater importance than living individuals). He gave me a 1st Class ticket and seat reservation on the Members' special train and asked where I would like to be on the course. My reply amused him greatly - I preferred a day return from Newbury to Lambourn to use during the meeting. An Inspector was assigned to me at Newbury to watch the trains assemble the race-goers and clear them afterwards. It was a real education and I have the photos to prove it.

It is amusing that the train waiting at Fraserburgh (page 29) is cosseted under an overall roof when, as the loco's cow-catcher suggests, it runs on unfenced track throughout much of its journey to Cairnbulg and St Combs. Westwards along the Buchan coast is Banff, and the train standing there (page 29) has conveyed a coffin from Tillynaught, the only passenger, presumably, other than Alan and myself!

Chard and Bicester (pages 34 and 28 respectively) are two other towns that boast two stations. Both have closed in Somerset, but the others remain, Bicester London Road now being a terminus for a service from Oxford, and North being served by new 'Turbo' trains on the Regional Railways route between Marylebone and Birmingham in competition with InterCity from Euston. Successors to the GWR and LNWR!

Llong was on the same line as the Hope exchange platforms and at the time of the photo (page 32) had a very meagre service of freight likely to come at any time. Provided there were semaphore signals to give warning of the train's approach, such locations were ideal for studying for examinations.

The notice at Norton-in-Hailes (page 32) must have been more in hope than certainty at the time, though with fax machines and the like, its remote position would not be so off-putting today.

Stamford station (page 33), apart from being a handsome structure, now houses a fine railway bookshop. Who knows - you might even find this publication there!

When I stand under the great curving roof of York station I am conscious of the, literally, millions of folk who must have waited there before me since it opened in 1877. There are few industries that can boast such long and continuous service, day and night, as the railways are able to do. I wonder who will buy or lease the station from the Railtrack Authority if, and when, it returns to the private sector. Who will succeed InterCity, BR (Eastern and previously North Eastern) of the public sector, and the LNER and NER of the private? There ought to be a wealth of experience to draw upon for running the place. I hope they abandon the recent innovation of actually charging people for parking when bringing customers to the train or picking them up. To have to pay in these circumstances hardly encourages rail travel.

**Madeley Market, Shropshire; 23 October 1960.**
**Whitwell, Isle of Wight; 18 April 1959.**
First, two examples of the neglected station. Madeley Market had been closed for more than eight years at the time of this photograph and the goods trains were to cease too some six weeks later. It was an intermediate station on the LNWR branch to Coalport in the Severn Valley and at the top of a steep incline; hence the notice on the left: 'Goods trains to Stop and Pin Down Brakes'.

It is to be hoped that railway privatisation, if it occurs, does not produce more complicated overlapping networks like those in South London, bequeathed to us by competing companies in the 19th century, nor duplicate branches such as that from Merstone to Ventnor in the Isle of Wight which, when it closed in 1952, was the first on the island to do so and left Whitwell station standing high and dry. *2300/1578*

**Rolleston Junction, Notts; MR '1P' 0-4-4T No 58065, 2.45 pm to Southwell.**
**Southwell, Notts; No 58065, 3.15 pm to Rolleston Junction, both 4 April 1959.**
Two pictures of the same train on the same day. Until 1959 it shuttled up and down, connecting the Midland line from Nottingham to Lincoln with Southwell, and was of particular interest to me as Rolleston Junction was the railhead for regular race meetings and they, after all, had stimulated my interest in railways, as already mentioned above. The branch continued beyond Southwell, though only for goods trains since 1929. These were augmented by two race specials on 1 April 1961, the handbill for which is reproduced here.

Rolleston is shown with Midland Railway wooden buildings, having MR notices in the windows on perforated metal. The BR sign is in Eastern Region blue. So is the station nameboard at Southwell. Here cast iron window frames contain fancy patterns. The signals owe their origins to the Midland Railway as does the quarter-milepost sign. This was my only outing in the company of both Hugh Davies and Geoff Hunt. They had driven north the previous day and I had caught them up in Melton Mowbray by using the 6.33 pm express from St Pancras (arrive 9.09 pm) with dinner on board. Now we were looking at railways in the Dukeries. *1555/1556*

BRITISH RAILWAYS

E 3015

**EASTER HOLIDAYS**

**SOUTHWELL RACES**

FIRST RACE — 2.30 p.m.
LAST RACE — 5.0 p.m.

**DAY EXCURSIONS**
TO
**ROLLESTON JUNCTION**
SATURDAY APRIL 1st

| OUTWARD JOURNEY | | | Return fares second class | RETURN JOURNEY | | |
|---|---|---|---|---|---|---|
| | a.m. | noon | s. d. | | p.m. | p.m. |
| Worksop .. ..dep. | .. | 12 0 | 7/- | **Rolleston Junction dep.** | 5 19 | 5 35 |
| | | p.m. | | | | |
| Whitwell .. .. „ | .. | 12 14 | 6/- | | | |
| Elmton & Creswell „ | .. | 12 20 | 5/6 | Southwell .. .. arr. | 5 27 | 5 41 |
| Langwith .. .. „ | .. | 12 26 | 5/- | Blidworth .. .. „ | 5 50 | 6 8 |
| Shirebrook (West) „ | .. | 12 32 | 4/9 | Mansfield (Town) .. „ | 6 13 | 6 30 |
| Mansfield Woodhouse „ | .. | 12 39 | 4/- | Sutton Junction .. „ | 6 33 | .. |
| Hucknall (Byron) .. „ | 11 45 | .. | 5/6 | Kirkby-in-Ashfield(East) | 6 39 | .. |
| Kirkby-in-Ashfield(East)„ | 11 59 | .. | 4/6 | Hucknall (Byron) .. „ | 6 50 | .. |
| | p.m. | | | Mansfield Woodhouse „ | .. | 6 40 |
| Sutton Junction .. „ | 12 4 | .. | 4/6 | Shirebrook (West) „ | .. | 6 45 |
| Mansfield (Town) .. „ | 12 22 | 12 48 | 4/- | Langwith .. .. „ | .. | 6 52 |
| Blidworth .. .. „ | 12 44 | 1 7 | 2/6 | Elmton & Creswell „ | .. | 7 0 |
| Southwell .. .. „ | 1 5 | 1 32 | 1/- | Whitwell .. .. „ | .. | 7 7 |
| **Rolleston Junction arr.** | 1 13 | 1 38 | | Worksop .. .. „ | .. | 7 20 |

If the races are cancelled and notice is given to this region in time to cancel these facilities the fares paid by intending passengers will be refunded on application

**PASSENGERS RETURN ON DAY OF ISSUE ONLY AS SHOWN ABOVE**

Tickets can be obtained IN ADVANCE at stations and travel agencies

Further information will be supplied on application to stations, offices, travel agencies or to Traffic Manager, Doncaster (Tel: 4031, Extn. 127); Traffic Manager, Farm Buildings Granville Road, Sheffield (Tel: 29611, Extn. 25) ; District Commercial Manager, Derby (Tel: 42442, Ext. 204) or Traffic Manager 26/28 Newland, Lincoln (Tel: 26352)

Children under three years of age, free; three years and under fourteen, half-fares, fractions of 1d. reckoned as 1d.

London, March 1961

Published by British Railways (Eastern Region) Printed in Great Britain Stafford & Co., Ltd., Netherfield, Nottingham

**Wells (Tucker Street), Somerset; LMS '2MT' 2-6-2T No 41296, Yatton-Witham, 10 October 1960.**

**Lodge Hill, Somerset; LMS '2MT' 2-6-2T No 41248, Yatton-Witham, 11 May 1963.**

The line from Yatton (Bristol/Exeter) to Witham (Westbury/Taunton) is illustrated in these two views. Alan and I have to wait some time at Wells, hence the picture. Do notice the postman with his mail-bags and the water column by the locomotive. Tucker Street station outlived the Somerset & Dorset Railway station in Priory Road, Wells, by nearly 12 years. Also note the wide space between the tracks caused by the need originally to provide for the broad gauge of 7 feet between the rails.

The past is also in evidence at Lodge Hill where the warehouse (of Bristol & Exeter Railway construction) has a door wide enough to accommodate the broad gauge. The station building has elaborate barge-boards. One of the posters advertises Ireland, but it looks very nice here to me! I'm driving up and down the line for pictures on a fine sunny day. *2261/2876*

**Bicester (London Road), Oxon; BR '4MT' 2-6-4T No 80081, 1 pm Bletchley-Oxford, 27 March 1959.**

**Upton-on-Severn, Hereford & Worcs; LMS '2P' 0-4-4T No 41900, 5.10 pm from Ashchurch, 21 March 1959.**

The common denominator of these two pictures is a terminus on a through line. Trains from Oxford now turn back at Bicester (London Road), but the tracks continue to Claydon and, on a care and maintenance basis, to Bletchley. The train from Ashchurch has to terminate at Upton-on-Severn, but until 1952 the tracks continued to Malvern.

On Good Friday 1959 the station at Bicester looks very dapper with its LMS 'Hawk's-eye' sign. A similar sign stands at Upton the week before where the station has a typical Midland Railway awning; the brickwork is extremely decorative. Earlier the same day I had taken a BBC tape-recorder aboard the train from Cirencester (Watermoor) to Andoversford (see the text on page 132) whilst Geoff had driven alongside, as it were, to pick me up there and head for Tewkesbury.

We stayed two nights in Winchcombe and I recall with affection a visit to the station on the Friday night to see the last train of the day - the 8.15 pm all stations from Honeybourne to Cheltenham Spa (St James's) - comprising a GWR '14XX' 0-4-2T and one 3rd Class coach. You could hear it coming for miles on the clear night air. It stopped. The guard stepped out. No one got on or off. He pulled a wire to extinguish the gas-lamp, waved his green lantern and the train set off, whistling as it entered the nearby tunnel. *1543/1538*

**Fraserburgh, Grampian; LMS '2MT' 2-6-0 No 46460, 10.30 am to St Combs, 21 May 1957. Banff, Grampian; CR '2P' 0-4-4T No 55221, 4.10 pm from Tillynaught, 2 June 1959.**
Two terminal stations on the Buchan coast. Fraserburgh closed in 1965 and Banff the year before.

It was my first visit to Scotland with Alan and the first page of our circular tour tickets took us from King's Cross to St Combs (hence the cow-catcher on the engine), where the porter started back on seeing it, and refused to take it from us whilst accepting its validity. We had taken three days to get there, having spent Sunday in Edinburgh and Monday travelling to Aberdeen by way of the Fife coast line through St Andrews.

Two years later we reached Banff! Do notice the drinking fountain on the left there with its two iron cups dangling below. *966/1693*

***Above*** **Foxfield, Cumbria; LMS '4MT' 2-6-4T No 42591, 1.00 pm Workington-Manchester (Victoria), 1 June 1960.**
Having alighted from the goods train from Coniston, Harry is sitting on the seat waiting to continue our journey to Ravenglass and then to Cockermouth and Carlisle. Note the oil lamps and the Furness Railway signs. The building is built of local slate. *2031*

*Above* **Wooler, Northumberland; LMS '2MT' 2-6-0 No 46476, 7.30 am goods from Tweedmouth.**
*Right* **Akeld, Northumberland; same train, both 28 May 1959.**
The same train on the same day and stations of similar architecture. There is little more to say, as I talk about the journey in the text (page 92). It's amazing, however, that 30 years after closure the station nameboard is still in situ at Akeld. There's a ground frame on the platform. *1651/1650*

*Left* **Kelmarsh, Northants; LMS '4MT' 2-6-4T No 42446, 1.45 pm Northampton-Market Harborough, 17 July 1959.**
This is probably the ugliest photo in the book. The station was to close five months later. Note the LMS sign and an LNWR milepost. Geoff Hunt and I were on the way to one of our Melton Mowbray weekends (see page 124 of the text). We had already taken pictures at Amersham and Fenny Stratford and before the end of the afternoon we would see the branch goods at Marefield Junction. The line through Kelmarsh was used by a sleeper between Euston and Scotland via the Settle & Carlisle for a while after the withdrawal of passenger trains. Following an overnight stay in Market Harborough I saw the up train before breakfast on 28 April 1972. I also ran one of my DMU charters this way from Clapham Junction to Derby and called at Clipston & Oxendon. *1733*

**_Right_ Stamford (Town), Lincs; LMS '2MT' 2-6-2T No 41227, from Seaton, 11 April 1964.**
I have always been led to believe that the existing superb station building at Stamford is topped by a weather-vane depicting the initials of the Syston & Peterborough Railway, predecessors of the Midland, but I have never checked it; certainly the bell tower would be a fitting place for it to crown. The push-and-pull service used to set down its passengers, then back across the up line and come forward to wait on the other side of the platform on the left. In this way connecting passengers had an easy change. The BR signs are in Eastern Region blue, and lighting is by gas. *3128*

**_Below right_ Cemmes Road, Powys; GWR '43XX' 2-6-0 No 6378, 3.45 pm Shrewsbury-Aberystwyth, 21 August 1959.**
The base for summer weekend photography on the Cambrian this time is at Carno where the closed station formed the basis of the Laura Ashley empire. Over the mountains the former junction for Dinas Mawddwy is a handsome building in local stone with elaborate barge-boards. Our meals were taken round a communal table at the B&B, so we dined in Newtown. *1797*

**_Above_ Llong, Clwyd; LMS '8F' 2-8-0 No 48253, westbound freight, 8 June 1965.**
**_Below_ Norton-in-Hailes, Shropshire; LMS '4MT' 2-6-4T No 42226, eastbound coal empties, 8 March 1963.**
Two rather forlorn-looking stations, the first closed in 1962, the other in 1956. Llong was probably built by a local contractor rather than the LNWR, whose signal still stands tall in the distance; the other is of the parent company, the North Stafford Railway. I saw the first train during a visit to take pictures of the last steam workings between Shrewsbury and Chester. The latter was taken soon after midday; we had just seen the southbound 'Pines Express' pass through Market Drayton and spent most of the day between there and Nantwich. *3462/2820*

GENTLEMEN
41227
STAFFORD

6378
GENTLEMEN

**Chard (GWR), Somerset; GWR '57XX' 0-6-0PT No 9671, 4.30 pm Taunton-Chard Junction, 5 August 1957.**
**GWR '74XX' 0-6-0PT No 7436, 9.34 am to Chard Junction, 20 February 1959.**
Chard was a typical Brunel country station, and little has changed in the time between the pictures except an increase in cobwebs and soot in the roof. The water tower stands in the distance, and just look at the mountains of mail bags and the ancient barrows. In the upper view Harry is adopting a characteristic pose with his macintosh over his arm. It's Bank Holiday Monday and we are on a circular tour travelling via Salisbury to Westbury and Witham; then to Yatton and doubling back somewhat to Taunton from where we will proceed to Chard Junction. We change again at Yeovil Junction in order to join the Pork Chop Train' (see the text on page 80) to get home. On the later visit I was in the car exploring the Somerset & Dorset as well as the GWR branches in the area. *1054/1503*

**Witham, Somerset; GWR '4575' 2-6-2T No 4597, 1.30 pm to Yatton, 5 August 1957.**
This photograph was taken on the same day as the first at Chard opposite; indeed, it is the preceding picture on the roll. The station is distinctive in having an overall roof just for the branch service - very much a Great Western environment. The porter has his hands on his hips, impatient to get rid of the train. *1053*

**Nelson & Llancaiach, Mid Glam; GWR '56XX' 0-6-2T No 5618, 9.35 am to Dowlais (Cae Harris), 18 May 1961.**
Great Western throughout - buildings, nameboard, footbridge and signal box - not to mention the train awaiting its connections on the Neath-Pontypool Road route over the Heads of the Valleys. The trip was a mixture of car and rail travel. *2411*

# 4. Junctions

I have already written about the importance of Newbury racecourse in my railway life. Newbury itself was significant too, as Harry, Alan and I changed there on our very first circular day tour.

We had met up at Farnham and gone by way of Alresford to Eastleigh. There we took the Didcot, Newbury & Southampton route to Newbury, going to and from Lambourn (again!) before taking the picture reproduced here on page 38. In those days it was Paddington for Weymouth as well as Waterloo, and the express is setting down local passengers for our train, on the right, which will take us to Devizes and Holt Junction. Then we started for home via Chippenham and Calne to Swindon. From there we had hoped to travel in the slip coach to Reading at the rear of the 'Merchant Venturer', but being Bank Holiday Monday, and large crowds on board, the express made the normal station stop much to our disappointment. I was able to remedy the omission later and travel to Bicester by slip coach when carrying out freelance work for the BBC Third Programme feature *On Railways*.

In connection with my activities for that programme, and on the initiative of the PRO of the Southern Region following lunch at the Charing Cross Hotel on 28 October 1960 (my first visit there!), I turned up at Paddock Wood, junction for Maidstone West and Hawkhurst, with my tape recorder, on 25 November. There I found a crowd of mainly retired railwaymen assembled in a large circle waiting for me to interview them about their days with the South Eastern & Chatham (and, as it happened, the London & South Western) railways. A most rewarding and interesting day - I even recorded a gentleman in his nineties recalling early days at Hawkhurst. I visited another at Cranbrook who remembered the opening day and hop-pickers' specials. Some of the recordings were used on the air. They and the remaining tape, which now constitute a valuable archive, have a special place in the collection of material I use at educational presentations and residential weekends.

Melton Constable (page 45) was at the very heart of the Midland & Great Northern Railway system. From its main platforms, said *The Times* on 10 July 1958, when its future was threatened, 'you can still hear the Burgh Parva cows at milking time, the marshalling yards end in meadowland'. The closure the following year is a lasting memorial to the folly and bigotry of the senior older railwaymen who were in charge at the time. They still remembered the days when it competed with their trains from Liverpool Street and now was a chance to settle old scores. I used to think such sentiments of mine far-fetched, but experience has taught me that I'm not that far from the truth. The civil servants in the road-dominated Ministry of Transport must have hardly believed their ears and good luck. Fancy keeping branch lines to Cromer, Sheringham, Fakenham (also since shut completely) and Wisbech (freight only since 1968), and closing this through route from the Midlands which also linked all the local profit centres (to use the conventional jargon!). It needed upgrading, it's true, but so did the A17 trunk road. Significantly that has now taken over the track-bed for miles, as well as the river crossing at Sutton Bridge. Just to motor on that road today and see the endless lines of heavy lorries to and from King's Lynn shows just how short-sighted the railwaymen were.

Passengers from Nottingham to King's Lynn, for example, were deliberately discouraged from travelling by train. The M&GN proper began at Bytham at an end-on junction with a branch from the Midland at Saxby, then on the main line from St Pancras to Nottingham but today carrying by the site only the service between Peterborough and Leicester. Here the train in our photo (page 45) was scheduled to wait for no less than 25 minutes (!) until its counterpart arrived from King's Lynn. Then the locomotives were exchanged (echoes of Moreton in Marsh, page 10) before travel resumed.

I have happier memories of The Mound (page 49), junction for Dornoch on the Inverness line to the far north of Scotland. Having said that, connections to Dornoch were few and far between. The last branch train left The Mound at five minutes past two in the afternoon when Alan and I were travelling there from Thurso on 27 May 1957, so we had to catch the bus. The bus stop stood on a piece of road that had been bypassed, so we placed ourselves and our luggage strategically where the two roads converged. Well that we did, for the bus would not have stopped otherwise. On board I heard Gaelic spoken for the first time, noticed that every seat had a different colour of upholstery and witnessed a cow being milked at the side of the highway. Next day the train back waited for us to photograph it at every station, except Cambusavie Platform where it had no reason to call, and deposited us at The Mound in time for the train on to Inverness. This too was to be significant. In those days the dining-car was attached to the rear of the northbound train from Inverness and provided breakfast. It was detached at The Mound and added to the southbound train. Hence we were able to take lunch, and it was the first time I recall the meal being served by a waitress on a train.

Alyth (page 48) was on the Caledonian main line from Perth to Aberdeen and you changed there for the branch to Alyth or to go south over the hill to Dundee. Twelve years after passenger traffic had ceased at Alyth, friends of mine were able to tread the derelict platforms when my first charter in Scotland, using two General Manager's saloons - one of which was said to be destined for the National Railway Museum - called there on 21 April 1979. We were hauled by a diesel locomotive so no picture can appear in this book.

Dunton Green and Bentley, junctions respectively for passengers to Westerham (until 1961) and Bordon (until 1957) (page 43), have become largely commuter stations. We used to nickname the Station Master at Westerham 'Mr 100%' for, quite rightly, he used to scrutinise our track permits before we wandered about the yard there for pictures. One day, on 20 June 1959 to be precise, he caught Harry Grenside and myself sitting in the rear driver's cab of the auto-trailer looking back towards Chevening, and we were unceremoniously told to leave. Quite right. We should have known better.

Reedsmouth (page 46), on the other hand, remains as much a Northumberland rural backwater as ever, thank goodness, and the tracks were lifted in 1964. When I visited it with Alan Lillywhite on 27 May 1959 we came on the goods train from Morpeth, which reversed at the junction before proceeding to Bellingham. At the time the area was fully signalled and controlled from the vast signal box, although there were only two trains each week. Dr Beeching should have rationalised this sort of situation rather than adopt the easy way out by closing it.

The timetables described Cairnie Junction (page 48) as an exchange platform. Certainly passengers were confined to an island between the tracks, which guaranteed a windswept sojourn in the middle of open country, and the meagre road access was from a country lane. I always associate the start of travel on this line with darkness. Trains for Inverness waited, as they still do, underneath the arches at Aberdeen and I used to look anxiously through the gloom and steam to ensure joining the right portion of the train because it was often divided *en route*. At Cairnie coaches by the coast to Elgin via Buckie would be detached. Others would go ahead to Keith and thence by way of Dufftown or, as now when there is no alternative, via Mulben.

Maud Junction (page 49) was some 26 miles due east of Cairnie at the point where the Buchan line from Dyce divided to run north to Fraserburgh and east to Peterhead respectively. Alan and I arrived there from the north on 21 May 1957 and had 35 minutes for a snack in the refreshment room. I recall homemade potted meat sandwiches served by a man who had just moved there from Osterley in Middlesex. We returned to Aberdeen from Peterhead by bus as far as Ellon and so were able to glance at the remains of the Boddam branch (closed entirely in 1945).

Just to remind ourselves that there are junctions without stations, I have included views of Worgret Junction, where the Swanage line diverged from the Waterloo-Weymouth route - and may well do so again under preservation - and Morebath Junction, of the Exe Valley line with the Taunton-Barnstaple route, closed finally in 1966 (page 42). In the interest of accuracy I should add that there was a Morebath Junction Halt, approached only by a cart-track, so sited as to be available to trains on both routes. Passengers, however, were advised to change at Dulverton (a station, incidentally, about two miles from the community of that name). There was also a Morebath station on the Taunton route.

Perhaps I can wrap up my notes about stations with three other memories. For names I think it is hard to beat 'Sibley's for Chickney and Broxted', for which separate arrival and departure times were always shown in the timetable. The trains calling there ran between Elsenham and Thaxted until 1952. I never had the good fortune to travel on that branch.

Altnabreac must be one of the most remote stations on the entire BR system. It is in Caithness and many miles from any public road. Trains stop only by request and, if you are advised not to alight at Llanbister Road without knowing where you are going next (page 16 above), how much more is this so at Altnabreac, where a barren landscape (afforested perhaps since my last visit) stretches to the far horizon. I had never stopped there, so on my fiftieth birthday this was remedied with the insertion of a five-minute photo stop into the schedule of another of my private charters involving the two General Manager's saloons. By this time we had added a kitchen and dining-car as well, and it must have been the first (and last?) time that passengers boarded at Altnabreac to be presented with a menu for a three-course luncheon. Later, on our return, at Helmsdale, I was to be feted by my guests with champagne and a cake especially made in Inverness. Very touching!

The last station on my list is Tynehead (closed 1969) on the Waverley route from Carlisle to Edinburgh. There the booking office and Post Office were one and the same. Ian and I called on 2 September 1965 to photograph the London express. According to the timetable only one train then called there and only in one direction. Asking the Post Mistress about this, she said there was a train the other way but it was never advertised. She then went on to say that each of us should contribute to railway finances and how about a single ticket to Heriot (the next station to the south) (page 164). To this we readily agreed and each ticket, at her suggestion, was dated for our respective birthdays! What a pity those happy, harmless days have gone. Are we really any better off financially as a result of all the closures?

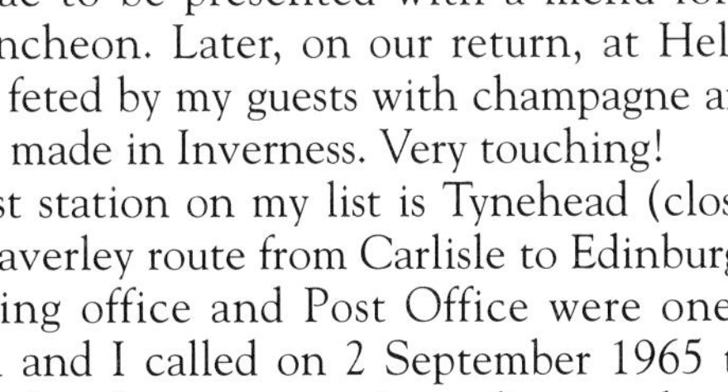

**Tiverton Junction, Devon; GWR 'Castle' 4-6-0 No 5011 *Tintagel Castle*, 9.10 am Liverpool-Paignton, 10 September 1959.**
**Newbury, Berks; GWR 'Hall' 4-6-0s No 6994 *Baggrave Hall*, 12.30 pm London (Paddington)-Weymouth, and No 4939 *Littleton Hall*, 1.50 pm to Bristol via Devizes, 2 April 1956.**
No question about main line status here, on the Great Western route to the West of England - milk churns on the up platform, oil sidings beyond and the Culm Valley branch to the right. Trains for Tiverton leave from behind the camera. The station has since been superseded by Tiverton Parkway at a motorway intersection further north. Significant, perhaps - we now expect to complete our journey from the main line by car. It's a Thursday and the usual three of us are having a day's leave - that's an excitement lost in retirement! The circular tour utilised the 7.49 am Surbiton to Guildford; 8.39 to Reading; 10.11 to Taunton; 12.10 pm to Tiverton Junction; 12.50 to Tiverton and 1.20 return; 1.40 to Hemyock and 3 pm return; 4.20 back to Taunton; 5.50 to Yeovil via Langport; and the 7.09 ('Pork Chop Train') to Surbiton.

For the benefit of the technically minded, I am told that the picture at Newbury illustrates the difference between the original and modified 'Hall' Class of locomotive, the latter having an extended frame and a plate frame bogie. The picture was taken on the first of our circular tours - the beginning of our journey through Britain by train. *1826/724*

**Ledbury, Glos; GWR '45XX' 2-6-2T No 4573, 12.15 pm from Gloucester (Central).**
**Same train shunting to siding, both 27 December 1958.**

Just after Christmas in 1958 and the weather was marvellous. Alan and I have arrived at Ledbury on the 9.45 am express from Paddington in time to see the train approach from Gloucester and pass those classic GWR signals before setting down at the up platform. In the lower picture, No 4573, having run round its train, will, as the 'theatre' route indicator on the shunt signal shows, propel the stock into the down siding out of the way of the connection to Worcester (which forms the subject of negative 1467!). Do notice the GWR gas-lamps and the newly erected '3-car' stop sign for DMUs. Having topped up with water from the column in the siding (which led almost to the west portal of Ledbury Tunnel), our train will emerge as the 1.30 pm back to Gloucester Central. We travel from there to Kemble, make sorties to Tetbury and Cirencester, and return home on the 5 pm to Paddington. *1466/1468*

**Builth Road (Low Level), Powys; LMS '2MT' 2-6-0 No 46511, 12.25 pm to Builth Wells, 18 April 1960.**
Consecutive pictures this time, of the empty stock of the 12.25 pm to Builth Wells, then the train ready to depart from Builth Road (Low Level). We have talked about exchange stations in the text (page 24), and this was a short working in connection with the 10.25 express from Swansea (Victoria), due upstairs two minutes earlier; the connection would have been guaranteed. At other times the Mid Wales train would have been popping down to Three Cocks Junction to bring back passengers from the Hereford/Brecon service. Do notice in the top left-hand corner of the upper picture the Cambrian signal and the spur which then enabled through workings from, say, Moat Lane Junction to Llandovery. I did not have the opportunity to use this. In the distance (lower view) is the equivalent junction signal; the tower contains a lift between the two stations. *1912/1913*

**Dulverton, Somerset; unidentified GWR '14XX' 0-4-2T, 5.25 pm to Exeter (St David's), and unidentified GWR '43XX' 2-6-0, 3.00 pm Ilfracombe-Taunton, 3 April 1961.**

**Grange Court Junction, Glos; GWR '43XX' 2-6-0 No 6330, 12.45 pm Gloucester (Central)-Hereford, 2 June 1962.**

Two more Great Western junctions, and I leave you to argue whether they are on main lines; a question of definition really. Dulverton is not at the actual point of junction of the Taunton/Barnstaple and Exe Valley routes, which is to the east at Morebath (see overleaf). It's not at Dulverton either, as the township is two miles to the north. It's Easter Monday and Harry, Alan and I are returning from a weekend in Cornwall. We left Launceston that morning and travelled via Tavistock and Plymouth to Exeter. There was time in hand, so we diverted by way of Dulverton to Taunton before going to Reading and home.

At Grange Court, where the Hereford line used to leave the Gloucester/Chepstow, it's the last day of a holiday in Wales. The nameboard here is an early GWR example on enamel, the station buildings dating back to the earlier South Wales Railway. Until the coming of the branch there was no community here and only a handful of cottages afterwards. It was nowhere, and I think that's splendid! You drove down the lane and, behold, a complete railway junction lay before you in the meadows. *2376/2690*

**Morebath Junction, Devon; unidentified GWR '43XX' 2-6-0, 12.20 pm Ilfracombe-Taunton, 26 February 1960.**
**Worgret Junction, Dorset; LSWR 'M7' 0-4-4T No 30052, 10.53 am Wareham-Swanage, 19 May 1963.**
Morebath Junction, referred to on the previous page, illustrates nicely the features of a country junction of two single-track lines. Note the pick-up apparatus for the tablet which gives the driver the right to proceed in safety; also the GWR catch-point sign, as the line is on a down gradient. (Catch-points are provided to stop any runaway wagons from endangering other trains; they deflect the wheels from the track on to adjacent land. There used to be a set on the climb from Surbiton to the viaduct at Hampton Court Junction. When installed, the land below the embankment was just meadow; I've often wondered whether the tenants of the council houses subsequently built in the field knew what might be in store for them from above their line of vision!) On this morning - a day of heavy rain - I had taken a BBC tape recorder on a locomotive from Cadhay Crossing to Ottery St Mary (on the Sidmouth branch) and back to describe the events surrounding the regular supply of fresh water to Mr Bedford, the crossing keeper, and his wife. Churns were taken to Ottery, filled and brought back. This was a common feature of railway life in those days.

I was in the New Forest early on the day of the Worgret picture. I had spoken at Southampton University the evening before and my hosts had to be up early for some reason or other and so I took advantage of this to enjoy the morning sun. The train being propelled to Swanage is made up of ex-Maunsell coaches converted to push-pull working. As the door of the signal box is open it's reasonable to suppose that the signalman is handing the driver the token for the single line ahead. The box is of LSWR origin with a hipped roof and windows of many small panes of glass. *1871/2881*

**Bentley, Hants; LSWR 'M7' 0-4-4T No 30027, 2.47 pm to Bordon, 17 August 1957.**
**Dunton Green, Kent; SECR 'H' 0-4-4T No 31279, 7.00 pm to Westerham, 20 June 1959.**
Two steam-worked branch lines connecting with the Southern Electric at junctions in the Home Counties (see text on page 37). These pictures were taken on Saturday afternoons after visits with Harry to the 'Little Thatch' restaurant near Godalming, a favourite haunt for lunch. He is standing at Bentley in company with Gerald Daniels, later BR organiser of steam specials, whom we chanced upon there. An ex-LSWR push-pull unit survives for the journey to and from Bordon.

It is ex-South Eastern & Chatham railmotor coaches, with air control push-pull gear and steam reverse, that make up the Westerham train we use as part of our trip to and from Hawkhurst. *1056/1713*

**Bere Alston, Devon; SR 'N' 2-6-0 No 31842, 11.38 am Plymouth (Friary)-Exeter (Central), 2 April 1961.**
It's the Cornwall weekend referred to in the caption for Dulverton above (page 41). On Easter Day the three of us took a circuit from Launceston, not an easy matter on a Sunday! We hired a taxi to Callington as the branch train was berthed there and began its shuttle to Bere Alston at that end, hence the connection to the train in the picture. Note the LSWR sign about crossing the line and, on the branch, a warning not to exceed 15 mph, presumably around the bend. The branch still survives as far as Gunnislake, mainly for Plymouth commuters, but the main line is no more except as a single track with trains reversing at Bere Alston. We travelled to Okehampton, had lunch, then west to Bude, returning to Launceston by bus. *2369*

**Long Melford, Suffolk; LNER 'B12/3' 4-6-0 No 61549, 2.01 pm Colchester-Cambridge, and GER 'J15' 0-6-0 No 65438, 3.15 pm to Bury St Edmunds, 10 June 1957.**
Long Melford on the Colchester (Mark's Tey)-Cambridge route was the junction for Lavenham and Bury St Edmunds until 1961, closing itself in 1967; note the tall wooden Great Eastern signal. It's Whit Monday and the circular tour of Alan and myself, starting at King's Cross at 9.20 am via Letchworth, continued at 1.34 pm from Cambridge via Haverhill, 3.15 from Long Melford (the train seen in the siding) and ended with the 4.37 from Bury St Edmunds which, because of the Bank Holiday, ran through to Liverpool Street, returning through Long Melford to Sudbury and reversing at Mark's Tey. It was scheduled to reach London at 7.17 pm. *1032*

**Saxby, Leics; LMS '4MT' 2-6-4T No 42137, 8.40 am Nottingham (Midland)-King's Lynn, 8 November 1958.**
**Melton Constable, Norfolk; LMS '4MT' 2-6-0 No 43095, 12.42 pm Yarmouth (Beach)-Peterborough (North), 4 August 1958.**
Two pictures of the Midland & Great Northern Joint Line service (see text on page 36) in the latter half of 1958. Saxby was visited on the first weekend with Geoff Hunt in Melton Mowbray, and the previous day we had passed our present editor's home near Raunds, Northants. There is a cattle dock in the background and several goods brake-vans in the adjacent yard.

We changed at Melton Constable as part of our coverage of the joint line, having come from Norwich (City) and going on to Wisbech North and Peterborough. It's about 2.30 pm on August Bank Holiday Monday. There are GN somersault signals in the background and a coaling stage on the right. *1452/1377*

**Reedsmouth Junction, Northumberland, NER 'J25' 0-6-0 No 65727, Morpeth-Bellingham freight, 27 May 1959.**
**Newton Stewart, Dumfries & Galloway; BR '2MT' 2-6-0 No 78026, freight to Whithorn, 27 May 1964.**
Two pictures taken on the same day but five years apart. Alan is enjoying the morning sunshine while the freight does some shunting at Reedsmouth where the signal box, of North British design, dominates the scene. The same company's signals grace the view. The little stand in the left foreground is where the signalman waits to hand the token for the single line to Bellingham. We have come from Morpeth along the line on the right and have now joined the defunct Border Counties from Hexham to Riccarton, closed in 1956. To my surprise there is electric lighting here.

At Newton Stewart another goods train awaits us for the journey down the Isle of Whithorn. The footbridge, carrying a handsome lamp, is by Oliver & Arrol of Edinburgh and dated 1880. The hills of Galloway line the horizon. I refer to the journey in the text (page 93). *1639/3208*

**Riddings Junction, Cumbria; LNER 'A2' 4-6-2 No 60535 *Hornet's Beauty*, 6.38 am Edinburgh (Waverley)-Carlisle, and LNER 'J39' 0-6-0 No 64932, 10.04 am to Langholm, 2 June 1960.**
**Roxburgh, Borders; LMS '4MT' 2-6-0 No 43138, freight from Jedburgh, and BR '2MT' 2-6-0 No 78049, 11.30 am St Boswells-Kelso, 18 July 1963.**

Two real country junctions. Riddings, which took its name from a nearby farm as there was nowhere else in the vicinity, still had a cobbled approach road to the nearest lane when I last visited it. In practice it was an exchange platform for passengers from Edinburgh to the terminus at Langholm as the picture illustrates. Most branch trains, sensibly, ran through from Carlisle and I was surprised that it closed, for trains always seemed well used. It was probably caught up in the Waverley route closure which I've always felt had its roots in party political considerations, egged on by a railway management who felt they had nothing to lose by its loss. It came into the same category as the M&GN (see the text on page 36). If it is true that traffic is viable by rail only if it travels some distance, as the pundits are always telling us, then traffic from the Border towns to the south should have come within that category.

Roxburgh had ceased to be a junction for passengers in 1948 when the Jedburgh branch closed, but the freight still ran and had to await the eastbound passenger before entering the single line to St Boswells. The station is oil-lit and has a North British signal box with sash windows. Someone has the pride to produce a floral display on the platform. I am in a friend's car which he had parked at Berwick on Tweed station, having sent me the spare key, so that I could alight from the London sleeper at about 5 am and drive into the country. Only in this way could I get to photograph the goods to Greenlaw on Leaderfoot Viaduct which ran early morning when the sun was in the right position. I was successful, but as it was diesel-hauled it cannot appear in this book. Hence at Roxburgh I began to feel that I had been up all night! *2040/2926*

***Above*** **Alyth Junction, Tayside; LMS Class '5' 4-6-0 No 44698, 5.30 pm Aberdeen-Glasgow (Buchanan Street), 31 August 1965.**
***Left*** **Cairnie Junction, Grampian; BR '4MT' 2-6-4T No 80121, 3.40 pm Aberdeen-Elgin via the coast, 2 June 1959.**
***Above right*** **Maud Junction, Grampian; LMS '2P' 4-4-0 No 40650, 1.40 pm to Peterhead, 21 May 1957.**
***Right*** **The Mound, Highland; BR '2MT' 2-6-0 No 78052, dining car to be attached to 8.35 am Wick-Inverness, and GWR '16XX' 0-6-0PT No 1648, 28 May 1957.**

Still in Scotland but now north of the Lowlands. Alyth Junction was 5 miles from Alyth to which ran a branch until 1951 (passengers), 1965 (goods). Passengers also changed here for Dundee until 1955, and trains ran up and over the main line with a spur towards Coupar Angus. Quite a substantial track layout in the middle of nowhere! It's a lovely evening and Ian Cantlon and I have come here during a few days in Forfar. The platforms are so low that it has been necessary to put concrete steps at the foot of the classic footbridge. There's quite a floral display on the platform, so someone loves the place.

Cairnie Junction (see the text on page 37) still has its Great North of Scotland Railway nameboard and fancy seats. We've come from Inverurie and are gong on to Tillynaught and Banff. I've also referred to Maud Junction and The Mound in the introductory text. Do notice the gas-tank wagon on the far right at The Mound, which will have been used to top up the restaurant cars when they were turned back to Inverness. *3511/1691/972/1015*

WAY OUT
40650
SC 3568 M

THE MOUND
78052

# 5. Secondary passenger lines

At last we have puffed out of the station and are on our way, first on the Central Wales line with its service from Shrewsbury to Swansea. An early morning train used to convey the mails and I well recall the Clerk of the former Knighton Rural District Council telling me how he kept an eye on the postcode lest this be changed, without the opportunity to comment, to Hereford (or some other) and the mail contract withdrawn from BR. Local government reorganisation swept away his really local authority in 1974 and the mail no longer travels here by rail.

Continuity of yet a different kind is assisted by another country junction, Penybont (page 2). Here, on the Central Wales, a line through a single-bore tunnel used to split into conventional up and down tracks as far as Llanbister Road. How the express trains would scurry along this relatively flat section through Dolau! I love the lower quadrant London & North Western Railway signal which must have guarded the junction for at least 60 years.

Another town with two stations, Brackley (Great Central, closed 1966) (page 53) brings back memories of a trip with Harry and Alan on 30 July 1958. We wanted to cover the entire M&GN before closure and in particular to use the through train that ran each weekday between Birmingham (New Street) and Yarmouth (Beach) via Bourne, as the timetable footnote pointed out, which had through coaches, detached at Melton Constable, for Cromer (Beach) and Norwich (City) respectively. So we set off from Euston and changed at Bletchley to reach Brackley (London & North Western, closed to passengers 1961). Those familiar with the town will realise that we had to climb the hill between the two stations. To encourage Harry to do this I promised him lunch on the train to Leicester (Central). This was the 12.15 pm from Marylebone via High Wycombe and the restaurant car attendant was delighted to oblige us in the hour which was occupied *en route*.

We then joined the 3.15 pm at Leicester (London Road) and travelled through to South Lynn, the same portion of route as covered by the refreshment car, where a shuttle service took us into King's Lynn and so home to Liverpool Street. I recall taking the second sitting of afternoon tea, between Bourne and Spalding. The car was at the back of the train, presumably for ease of attaching and detaching, and rocked about without mercy as we sped along the deteriorating track over the soft fens. The attendant had put layers of paper napkins on the table-cloth but still the spilt tea seeped through!

Barnetby (page 53) is on the original Great Central line from Manchester to the Lincolnshire coast at Grimsby/Cleethorpes. Unlike the GCR's London Extension, this has survived and is now probably the least modernised junction on BR with its gantries of semaphore signals and large signal box. Every time the Government economises, these outdated features soldier on.

Daggons Road station, served by trains between Salisbury and Bournemouth until 1964, and situated in the village of Alderholt, was so called to avoid confusion with Aldershot. I took the picture you see on page 55 on my first visit, made by bicycle which had been carried on the train from Surbiton to Brockenhurst and again from there to West Moors; it was eventually taken home from Salisbury. I went to show the booking clerk my track permit and found him in an office begrimed with soot which had to be lit, even on a sunny day, by Tilly oil-lamp. It cannot have been painted for years.

Later I must have cycled faster than at any other time in my life. I was determined to photograph the 5.37 pm to Bournemouth West at Downton, and at Alderholt Junction the train which it crossed at Fordingbridge. Six unfamiliar hilly miles in barely half-an-hour with a wrong turning at the end. I made it - just!

Berkeley South Junction (page 57) was used mainly when the Severn Tunnel was closed for maintenance and trains had to be diverted, with light-weight engines, over the Severn Bridge between Lydney and Sharpness. The Cardiff-Portsmouth service was one of the most affected.

Irthlingborough (page 60), on the Northampton-Peterborough line, must have had the biggest tannery, or equivalent, near the station. I had no wish to remain there longer than necessary.

Dent (page 61) on the Settle & Carlisle brings to mind a luncheon to which I was invited by the General Manager, Jim O'Brien, in the Officers' Mess at Euston on 7 January 1982. There was excitement during the sweet course when someone diagonally opposite across the table suddenly cried 'I know who you are! You chartered a train which called at Dent and you failed to pay the fee due to the National Park Authority for restoring the platforms there.' This outburst came as a total surprise to me, as did the news of the alleged debt! I had certainly stopped the saloon of the GM (Eastern) there on 22 April 1978, but had no knowledge of the sequel. Obviously the gentleman in question had a good memory.

**Barmouth Bridge, Gwynedd; GWR '45XX' 2-6-2T No 4549, 9.00 am Machynlleth-Barmouth, 11 May 1958.**
During a fortnight's holiday in Wales with Alan we spent a traditional seaside weekend in Barmouth and strolled down to the viaduct on the Sunday morning to take this picture soon after breakfast. *1273*

**Llanbister Road, Powys; LMS Class '5' 4-6-0 No 45422, 12.25 Swansea (Victoria)-Shrewsbury.**
**LMS '4MT' 2-6-4T No 42307, 2.50 pm Shrewsbury-Swansea (Victoria), both 19 August 1959.**
I sense that there may be more pictures in this book of the Central Wales than of any other railway. If so it's because it is one of my favourite lines and runs through superb scenery. Today it is well maintained and cared for due to the interest of the Prince of Wales and of the parish councils who take a pride in the many unstaffed halts and keep them clean and tidy. Do notice the oil lamps and the LNWR signs. *1782/1783*

**Brackley (Central), Northants; LMS '6P' 4-6-0 No 45573 *Newfoundland*, 2.38 pm London (Marylebone)-Nottingham (Victoria), 16 March 1963.**
**Barnetby, Humberside; LNER 'B1' 4-6-0 No 61111, 2.12 pm Cleethorpes-Sheffield (Victoria), 3 August 1959.**
Two stations on the Great Central. Brackley, a typical island station on the London Extension, is very clean and tidy but has little traffic in the yard. I'm spending the day in the car on the GC and take seven pictures.

The other station, on the original main line, still boasts a GC signal on the extreme right of the picture. Harry, Alan and I have arrived here from Worksop. *2848/1757*

**Semley, Wilts; SR 'U' 2-6-0 No 31633, 12.48 pm Templecombe-Salisbury.**
**Andover Town, Hants; LSWR 'M7' 0-4-4T No 30033, 10.42 am Andover Junction-Eastleigh, both 19 February 1959.**

Two pictures taken the same morning en route to the West of England, and in February when the roads were quieter and the skies contemplative. The Southern Region timetable contained five pages devoted to bus connections from its main line, and a regular service was shown between Semley and Shaftsbury along the A350. The station closed in 1966 and passengers are now taken on to Gillingham along a single track. The train is composed of Bulleid stock and there are cattle wagons in the yard. The cold winter morning comes across in the photo.

Andover has changed out of all recognition since the station, on the Test Valley line, shared by the Southampton/Cheltenham service, was swept away. Concrete fittings are much in evidence as are the signals which were linked to the level crossing over the main road and the approach to Andover Junction, which survives. *1497/1495*

**Daggons Road, Dorset; LSWR 'T9' 4-4-0 No 30300, 10.04 am Bournemouth (West)-Salisbury, 1 October 1955.**
**Nursling, Hants; SR 'U' 2-6-0 No 31802, 2.00 pm Cheltenham (Lansdown)-Southampton (Terminus), 7 September 1957.**
The lower picture shows a train that has passed through Andover Town earlier. It has come from Cheltenham with Great Western rolling-stock, and the locomotive carries express code headlamps rather than route indication discs.

I have already spoken about the picture at Daggons Road in the text (page 50). *642/1085*

**Cheltenham Spa (Malvern Road), Glos; SR 'U' 2-6-0 No 31809, 1.52 pm Cheltenham (St James's)-Southampton (Terminus), 27 December 1960.**
**Midsomer Norton South, Avon; BR '4MT' 2-6-0 No 76026, Bath (Green Park)-Bournemouth (West) local, 27 February 1965.**
Two more cross-country trains. The first is a descendant of the one overleaf at Nursling, just beginning its mammoth slow journey to the coast. I'm about to get on board and looking forward to a completely relaxed afternoon passing through the Cotswolds, the Upper Thames, the chalk downland around Marlborough and finally the Test Valley. The picture was taken during the brief period prior to withdrawal when these trains used Cheltenham St James's station rather than Lansdown. Look at the old-fashioned Tannoy for announcements.

The second train is going south over the parallel Somerset & Dorset line. I'm staying with Ian at North Curry, handy for pictures of this route, and again it is February. The train has an S&D headcode and is made up of ex-Great Western and BR Mark 1 stock. *2317/3363*

**Breidden, Powys; GWR '43XX' 2-6-0 No 5331, 3.45 pm Shrewsbury-Aberystwyth, 15 May 1958.**
Breidden station (closed 1960), between Shrewsbury and Welshpool, began life as Middletown, was renamed Middletown Hills in 1919 and again in 1928. Clearly it served little. At the time of the photo the signal box too was switched out and all trains were signalled through the down line. The train is made up of three Great Western coaches and one BR Mark 1 vehicle. *1302*

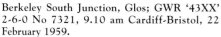

**Berkeley South Junction, Glos; GWR '43XX' 2-6-0 No 7321, 9.10 am Cardiff-Bristol, 22 February 1959.**
The journey which started with a photo at Andover Town has now brought Geoff and myself to Severnside. As the Severn Tunnel is closed for maintenance, this train has passed above the waters over the Severn Bridge (page 152), now available to Blue route engines within Great Western categorisation but restricted to Yellow route engines until a few years earlier. There is a milk tank at the back of the train and a Midland signal for the down main line. *1518*

**Luffenham, Leics; LTSR '3P' 4-4-2T No 41975, 2.57 pm Seaton-Stamford (Town), 18 July 1959.**
**Ellesmere, Shropshire; GWR '14XX' 0-4-2T No 1423, 2.40 pm to Wrexham (Central), 16 May 1958.**
The common feature is the push-and-pull train, the one at Ellesmere being about to set out for Wrexham Central, the other midway on its journey from Seaton (Leicestershire) to Stamford, having just entered the tracks from Melton Mowbray. I don't know who it is leans out of the LMS Brake 2nd at Luffenham but the line's Midland origins are clearly identified by the junction signals and ground signal. There is an LMS 'Hawk's-eye' sign on the platform, which is still so low that steps are provided to facilitate access to the train. Why there was a through line eastbound only, I cannot say.

The fine station building at Ellesmere housed the offices of the Oswestry, Ellesmere & Wrexham Railway Company and the fine nameboard listed the various places served by the branch. There is a parachute tank for water supplies. *1745/1305*

**Brecon, Powys; LMS '2MT' 2-6-0 No 46526, 1.20 pm to Moat Lane Junction, 20 May 1961. Drws-y-Nant, Gwynedd; BR '4MT' 4-6-0 No 75026, 2.35 pm Barmouth-Birkenhead (Woodside), 27 July 1963.**
The station at Brecon was shared by trains operated by the Brecon & Merthyr, Cambrian, Midland and Neath & Brecon companies, so it was possible to run services in harmony. It's Whitsuntide and as it is a Saturday I've come from Carmarthen using the additional train that ran each week from Neath (Riverside). A lady had joined at Aberbran and was knee-deep in grass on the platform! I'm going on to Newport and Cardiff so as to travel to Llanwit Major the following day. Note that the station is gas-lit.

To reach Drws-y-Nant I had driven from London the previous day, picking up David Lawrence off the evening train at Newtown, staying in Llandinam and going on over the mountains on Saturday morning. *2422/2964*

***Right*** **Garsdale, Cumbria; 27 May 1960.**
***Below right*** **Dent, North Yorks; LMS Class '5' 4-6-0 No 45126, 3.35 pm Bradford (Forster Square)-Carlisle, 23 April 1965.**
Is the Settle & Carlisle a main line or a secondary route? Although the view of Garsdale contains no train I'm sure it's worthy of inclusion as the Midland signal in the right background (worked from a Midland box) shows that the Wensleydale branch to Northallerton was still then in situ. There is an oil-lamp on the platform and masses of wires on the telegraph poles. Alan can also be seen; we have just arrived by taxi from Hawes and it's a miracle that we have made the connection.

I took the picture at Dent during a week's stay at my favourite B&B - Close House, Giggleswick - with the Hargreaves. My first visit was in 1964, having observed from the OS map that the Morecambe line ran through the grounds of the farm, and I have returned consistently ever since! I even made some tape recordings from an upstairs window with the microphone on a boom. If you stop a charter train at Dent you need to pay a parking fee (see the text on page 50). *1992/3428*

**Broom North, Warks, LMS '4MT' 2-6-0 No 43033, 2.26 pm Evesham-Birmingham (New Street), 11 June 1962.**
**Irthlingborough, Northants; LMS '6P/5F' 2-6-0 No 42969, 12.38 pm Peterborough (North)-Northampton (Castle), 18 April 1964.**
The Broom picture is referred to in the text on page 68. Broom North (an LMS box dating from 6 May 1934) is at the extreme western end of the Stratford on Avon & Midland Junction Railway, which set out from Blisworth on the West Coast Main Line and Ravenstone Wood Junction on the Midland route from Bedford to Northampton, and enables trains to proceed towards Birmingham. A spur giving direct connection to Evesham was provided from 27 September 1942 and can be seen in the background. The signalman has left the door open whilst walking down to exchange tokens with the driver for the various single-line sections.

The ornate station building at Irthlingborough was built by the London & Birmingham Railway, while the signal box dates back to the London & North Western Railway. *3052/3132*

GARSDALE

45126

# 6. Passing places

To complete our tour of the M&GN we had to cover the Norwich (City)-Melton Constable and Sutton Bridge-Peterborough (North) sections, a series of mainly single lines with passing loops. This we did on Bank Holiday Monday, 4 August 1958, and arrived at Wisbech (North) (page 64) soon after four o'clock. Always on the alert for potential photo opportunities, I noticed from Bradshaw that not only did we pass there a local to King's Lynn, which was due to enter the loop after our arrival, but that another train set out for Peterborough about a quarter of an hour after our express had left. Thus two views could be obtained. This second train, which we joined, was another example of the mismanagement of the service. Originally there had been five intermediate stations towards Peterborough and, naturally, to allow the express to proceed non-stop, the second service gave more local passengers a connection. However, three of the stations had been closed the previous year, so it was no surprise to us to find that we had the four coaches of the second train to ourselves!

The loop at Crymmych Arms brings back happy memories of the Cardigan branch (closed completely in 1963). The day the picture (page 66) was taken was sunny from morning to night and we spent it driving up and down the valley taking a selection of pictures which I cherish. The line twisted about so much to ease gradients that it was easy to see the same train twice whilst driving in a responsible manner. On board the train, on 9 May 1958, we were puzzled by the long station stop at Rhydowen Halt until we looked out of the window to find the engine driver picking rhubarb from his adjacent allotment. On that occasion we arrived at Whitland by car from Newcastle Emlyn so tight for the departure of the branch train that we parked it hastily in a yard by the platform. On our return from Cardigan we found the yard gate locked. The signalman leaned out of his box with the keys and asked us not to park in there again!

Llangwyllog with its loop, on the Anglesey Central Railway, is of more recent significance to me. After retirement I was invited by Colin Driver (Director, Freight) to contribute to the BR newspaper now known as *Trainload Express* a series of photographs in the 'then and now' style. This I greatly welcomed. It was stressed that where possible I should concentrate on lines used exclusively by the then Freight Sector. The branch from Gaerwen (between Bangor and Holyhead) to Amlwch seemed an ideal candidate, particularly as in my view it must have a limited life, being retained to connect with a factory that apparently puts lead into petrol. So I thought that I would revisit Llangwyllog to compare the mixed freight in the picture you see (page 65) with its modern counterpart. This I did on 18 April 1989. It proved difficult to find. Trevor Owen and I actually drove over the bridge adjacent to the station without noticing it through the undergrowth. Eventually we found the station approach and located the position at which I had previously stood. No longer a loop (though the ground frame remained under the bracken) we watched the Class '47' haul its wagons through on a murky morning, largely man-made.

On reaching Gaerwen the signalman told us we were lucky, for, unusually, the loco would return for more wagons and was bound to be delayed near Amlwch because it would arrive there as the factory closed for lunch. True to his word, this enabled me to get a second picture at Llangwyllog in the sunshine, which was duly published. I got the impression that the newspaper staff never appreciated the time and knowledge involved in securing such a picture. It's much easier to stand on the platform-end at Crewe and photograph the first freight to come by, but that has never been my style. I needed to obtain and consult a Working Timetable in the first place, to stay somewhere overnight because the only train of the day ran early morning, and to hang about when it failed to run to time. Generally speaking, however, they were very helpful and I was sorry when the series was discontinued.

Two other loops worthy of particular mention lay in the Brecon Beacons, used by freight to Merthyr and passenger trains to Newport. Pentir Rhiw (Pant y Rhiw on the Ordnance Survey 1-inch map) had been submerged in the Talybont Reservoir but its station remained, used, according to the signalman there, by one lady a week travelling to and from Brecon market. At the summit loop at Torpantau (page 67) stood just an isolated signal box and station house. Due to successive reductions in the service the signalman there, on the second shift, sat idle for many hours between trains. One of them, who had to motor-cycle home miles down the valley after the last train had cleared his section, told me that in the winter the darkness and intense cold could be oppressive despite his phone link along the line and his coal fire. The only sound was the rattling of the levers in the frame as sheep tripped over the point rodding and signal wires outside.

Passing places on single lines can be very frustrating. When the Central Wales was undergoing one its severest economies, the loop was removed at Llandrindod Wells station but retained a few hundred yards north at a manned level crossing. On more than one occasion I have sat there for half an hour, within sight of the platform, unable to alight until the late-running eastbound train has come along (with associated crew change sometimes). I'm pleased to say that this has now been put right.

**Garneddwen Halt, Gwynedd; GWR 'Manor' 4-6-0 No 7821 *Ditcheat Manor*, 2.35 pm Barmouth-Ruabon, 26 May 1962.**
The porter at Llandrillo station was surprised when I drew up in my Morris Minor, asked if I could park there for the day, and when, with Harry and Alan, we all produced circular tour tickets for a trip utilising the train from which this picture is taken; we were staying in the village.
The scene includes a typical GWR halt, opened on 9 July 1928. *2653*

**Wisbech (North), Cambs; LMS '4MT' 2-6-0 No 43109, 3.42 pm Peterborough (North)-King's Lynn, and LMS '4MT' 2-6-0 No 43086, 4.35 pm to Peterborough (North).**
**LMS '4MT' 2-6-0 No 43086, 4.35 pm to Peterborough (North), both4 August 1958.**
I discussed the operation of these trains on page 62. The one on the left contains fruit vans and a North Eastern Railway four-wheeled passenger brake-van. Note the gas lamps and the staff; there were also GNR somersault signals here. Having come from Liverpool Street via Yarmouth (Beach), the usual trio had time to take the 5.40 pm from Peterborough North to Stamford, the 6.22 to Seaton and the 6.56 from there to Peterborough (East) before joining the King's Cross express at 8.02 pm. Harry's ticket cost substantially more than Alan's or mine; on examination we found that he had been routed to Devon and back, so he claimed a refund. *1381/1380*

**Ballindalloch, Grampian; GNR 'K2' 2-6-0 No 61782, eastbound freight, and unidentified BR '2MT' 2-6-0, 10.10 am Craigellachie-Boat of Garten, 23 May 1957.**
The working timetable showed that we were due to pass a goods at Ballindalloch, and there it was waiting outside the station as we drew in. Out of the compartment, carefully leaving the door open for my return, up on to the footbridge and, hey presto, the picture that you now see. I'm still on my first visit to Scotland and en route from Aberdeen, via Craigellachie and the Spey Valley, to Pitlochry. 988

**Llangwyllog, Gwynedd; BR '2MT' 2-6-0 No 78058, Amlwch-Bangor freight, 21 May 1962.**
The story of Llangwyllog is told in the text on page 62. There is an LNWR seat, including the station name, and a signal of the same origin. An open ground frame has its instruments in the office. 2635

**Tenby, Dyfed; GWR 'Manor' 4-6-0 No 7825 *Lechlade Manor*, 9.50 am Whitland-Pembroke Dock, 19 May 1961.**
**Crymmych Arms, Dyfed; GWR '16XX' 0-6-0PT No 1648, 6.16 pm Whitland-Cardigan, and GWR '45XX' 2-6-2T No 4557, freight from Cardigan, 31 May 1962.**
A Western Welsh low-bridge bus is waiting for the passengers from the train at Tenby, now on its way to Pembroke Dock. We crossed one coming the other way at Manorbier, took the Hobb's Point ferry from Pembroke to Neyland and proceeded from there as described in the text (page 148).

The Tenby branch left the main line to West Wales at Whitland. Trains also set off from there for Cardigan, and the evening working has reached Crymmych Arms where it is passing the second goods of the day. *2415/2674*

**Torpantau, Powys; GWR '2251' 0-6-0 No 2218, 12.15 pm Brecon-Newport, and unidentified loco, 11.15 am Newport-Brecon, 20 August 1959.**
I have written at length about Torpantau (page 62). Do notice all the apparatus adjacent to the signal box for exchanging single-line tablets. *1789*

**Ffestiniog, Gwynedd; GWR '74XX' 0-6-0PT No 7442, Blaenau Ffestiniog-Bala freight, and GWR '74XX' 0-6-0PT No 7414, Bala-Blaenau Ffestiniog freight, 12 May 1958.**
The signal box at Ffestiniog bears an old-style name dating from the very opening - 'Festiniog Station Signal Cabin'. Alan has left the brake-van to take a picture of the passing goods. *1281*

# 7. Passenger branch lines

At the time of the photograph at Braunston (opposite) there were only three trains each way per day. Not surprising perhaps but, unbelievably, only the same number served the expanding town of Daventry. No wonder the line closed to passengers in 1958, for most of the trains, from Leamington, turned back at the remote country station known as Napton & Stockton, three miles from Napton and over a mile from Stockton. Why? I have never understood this for the folk of Daventry would have welcomed a regular train to the West Midlands conurbation or Northampton had it been provided. As it was, the trains stood at Napton almost long enough to make the round trip to Daventry, the last even returning north empty stock! The most notable exception, however, one of the three through trains to Weedon on the West Coast Main Line, continued to and from Northampton by reversal at Blisworth. We used it on 7 April 1958, and the porter at Leamington Spa (Avenue) was so pleased to be able to tell us it was a through service. It was held a long time on the branch at Weedon, but when given the road on to the West Coast Main Line it was propelled like the clappers to Blisworth and shot into the bay there, hotly pursued by a Euston express.

The scene at Ashcott & Meare (page 71) on the original section of the Somerset & Dorset is reminiscent of Ireland. For some reason the pre-cast concrete gents toilet there stood remote from the platform on boggy ground.

The picture at Ripple (between Ashchurch and Upton-on-Severn) (page 72) is of a train officially standing there for eight minutes. For years the timetable explained at footnote 'A' that it arrived at 5.49 pm and left at 5.57 pm. Why? There was only the one train in steam on the branch. Perhaps there had once been a loop on the single line and it had passed another train there. I have yet to discover. The station has another claim to fame, however, in being near a bridge over the M50 Ross Spur Motorway that was provided just before the line closed in 1963.

The train at Hinton (page 73) is one of only a handful to run that way from Birmingham (New Street) to Ashchurch. On Bank Holiday Mondays, however, the service north of Evesham was transformed to carry all the day-trippers. Such a day was the obvious one to take pictures, so I drove along the line on Whit Monday 1962. Imagine my consternation when I discovered that the special leaflet I had picked up at St Pancras contained timings substantially different from those supplied at Evesham. Neither mentioned that some trains ran to and from Ashchurch.

At Tenbury Wells (page 74) we have just alighted from the push-pull train from Ludlow, involving reversal at Woofferton, and are awaiting the Bewdley train which has been extended to Kidderminster to assist through passengers returning home on Easter Monday 1960. I had written to the Station Master there stressing the need for us to catch the service from Stourbridge Junction that would be coupled to the Paddington express at Worcester (Shrub Hill). As we rounded the curve in sight of Kidderminster station we were held at a signal and could see congestion ahead. Eventually we were pulled forward into the platform behind another train and could hear loudspeaker announcements urging us to hurry over the footbridge. There a porter stood holding open the door of a 1st Class compartment (we usually travelled 2nd but obviously certain assumptions had been made about someone who wrote letters!) and we were bundled in as the train moved off.

Farrington Gurney Halt (page 76) lay on the North Somerset line between Bristol and Radstock. By the time I came to run my second charter train, a Swindon-built DMU, on a circuit from Salisbury, in March 1968, it had been closed to all traffic for four years, but the track had not been lifted. Imagine my excitement when I was informed by the Western Region that it was to be reopened and that we could go that way if we wished; also, because this provided us with unexpected extra time, would we like to go to and from Cheddar as well? We did! You cannot please everyone, however. The itinerary amended from the one first advertised omitted a little-used spur near St Philip's Marsh and I received an irate letter about this from a would-be traveller!

I obtained the picture at Burrator Halt (page 79) only because of the co-operation of the guard. He held the Princetown train whilst I ran out and took it. This was in the very early days of my new interest in railways and I had had to convince my two friends, with whom I was on holiday, that it would be a nice ride and a change from the car.

Finally, may I turn our attention to the Fairford branch on which we have views at Cassington and Lechlade (page 78). My first visit was on 23 June 1957, and because it was a Sunday the only eastbound train did not run until the early evening on our way home. Alan and I therefore travelled from Surbiton on a special that ran direct to Windsor & Eton (Riverside) via the now defunct curve at Staines; then on the Western to Slough, Henley and Swindon; and by bus to Fairford. It was a glorious sunny evening in the valley of the Upper Thames and the crop was already ripening golden by the lineside. The one bizarre event was the sight of American airmen pointing their machine guns at me as I took the air from the carriage window alongside Brize Norton airfield.

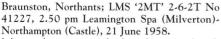

**Christ's Hospital, Sussex; LMS '2MT' 2-6-2T No 41299, 3.23 pm Horsham-Guildford, 13 May 1965.**
A natural switch from a country junction to a branch line as the train from Horsham enters the single track towards Guildford and leaves Christ's Hospital where the guard has had to look from both sides of the train for passengers prior to departure (as at Horsted Keynes). Sunday School Treat specials from Surbiton to the coast, steam hauled in my day, used to reverse here and everyone received an Eldorado ice-cream in a non-electrified platform line. I am reminded of an article I had published in *Trains Illustrated* in November 1956 (when I had material in *The Railway Magazine* and *Railway World* too) about the timetable of trains through Cranleigh; I was let loose at Porchester Road amid the archive Bradshaws so that I could consult as many as possible. *3444*

**Braunston, Northants; LMS '2MT' 2-6-2T No 41227, 2.50 pm Leamington Spa (Milverton)-Northampton (Castle), 21 June 1958.**
I discuss the service on this branch at some length opposite. Do notice the oil-lamp on the signal box (which in reality is only a ground frame). The train has one LMS purpose-built push-and-pull coach coupled to a Brake 2nd. *1329*

**Hatherleigh, Devon; LMS '2MT' 2-6-2T No 41314, 8.52 am Torrington-Halwill Junction.**
**Hole, Devon; same train, both 18 May 1959.**
Two pictures of the same train, on which I am travelling, between Torrington and Halwill. The branch was not built until 1925 and there was virtually no passenger traffic. Obviously it had to be included in our UK itinerary and the timetable was so sparse that we have travelled sleeper from Paddington to Exeter in order to connect with this service. It's a Whit Monday and Harry, Alan and I go south to Wadebridge and Bodmin Road before returning home. *1620/1619*

**West Pennard, Somerset; LMS '2MT' 2-6-2T No 41296, 9.45 am Highbridge-Templecombe, 21 February 1959.**
**Ashcott & Meare, Somerset; LMS '2MT' 2-6-2T No 41232, 9.55 am Evercreech Junction-Highbridge, 27 February 1965.**
The original purpose of the Somerset & Dorset was to carry coal between the Bristol Channel and the English Channel. These two pictures illustrate the area east and west of Glastonbury. The train at West Pennard, where a signal box survives, though disused, must be an unbalanced working as it is twice the normal length.

The scene at Ashcott is reminiscent of Southern Ireland, and the concrete nameboard jars against the old S&D signal. *1513/3361*

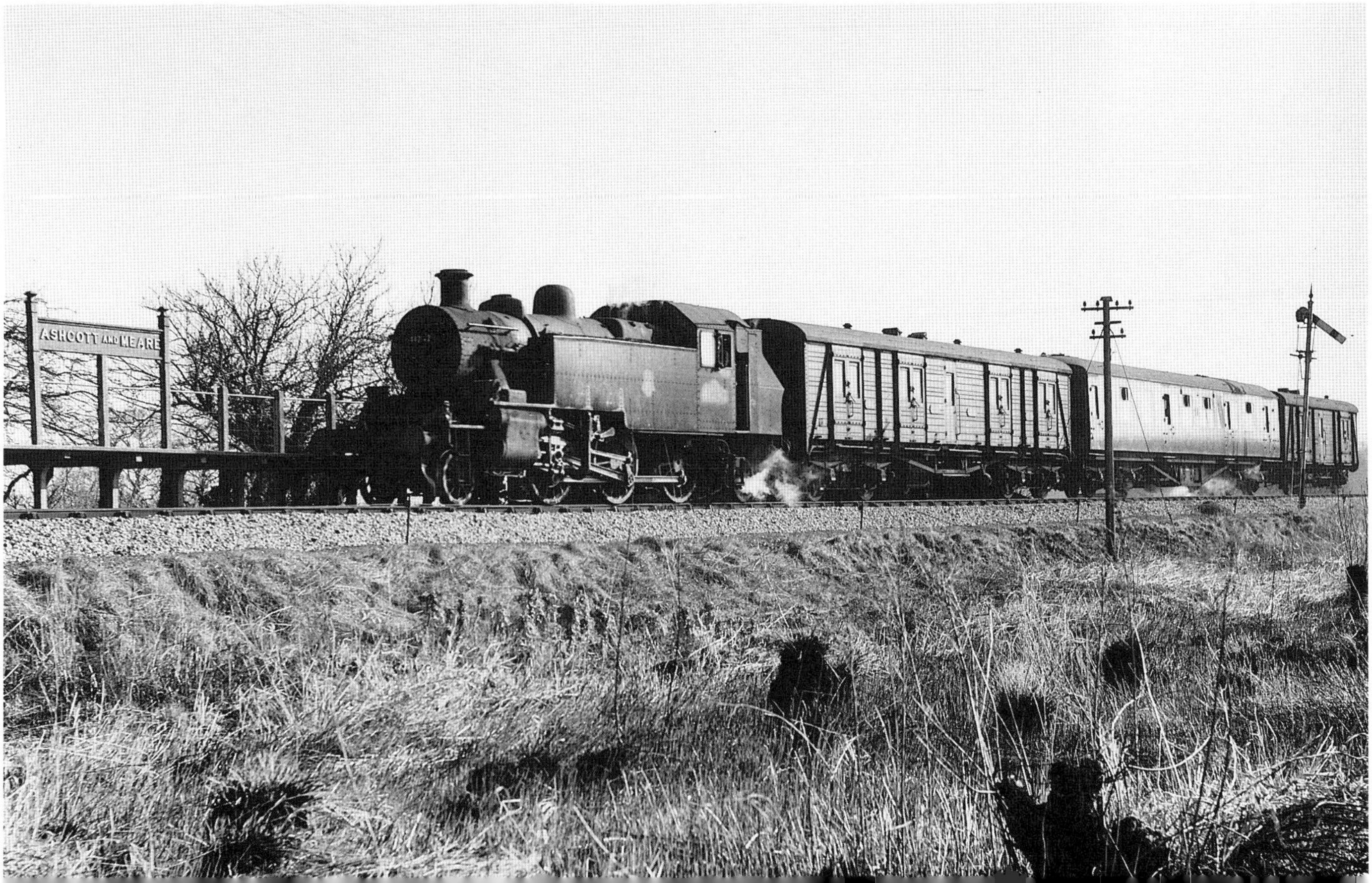

**Ripple, Hereford & Worcs; LMS '2MT' 2-6-0 No 46401, 5.45 pm Upton on Severn-Ashchurch, 6 May 1958.**
**Tewkesbury, Glos; LMS '2P' 0-4-4T No 41900, 4.20 pm to Ashchurch, 21 March 1959.**
I comment on the upper picture in the text on page 68. There is an LMS nameboard on the platform and Midland Railway diagonal fencing. Mainly in the car, Alan and I have visited Ballingham, Symonds Yat, Speech House, Staple Edge, Soudley, Severn Bridge and Bullo Pill for photos before joining the train at Tewkesbury for a return to Upton.

Back again the following year with Geoff, we've been to Foss Cross and Greenway Halt for photos before arriving in Tewkesbury. The loco is one of a batch of ten built in 1932 - as old as me! I love the gas-lamp in the foreground. *1247/1536*

*Above right* **Hinton, Hereford & Worcs; LMS '2MT' 2-6-0 No 46527, Birmingham (New Street)-Ashchurch, 19 May 1962.**
*Right* **Erwood, Powys; LMS '2MT' 2-6-0 No 46523, 9.55 am Moat Lane Junction-Brecon, 18 April 1960.**
The class of locomotive is the link between these two views. The picture at Hinton, showing its Midland Railway signal box and goods shed, was the first on a fortnight's holiday in Wales. Others that day were at Arley (pre-preservation) and Lightmoor, and Alan and I stayed overnight at Ditton Priors before heading for Menai Bridge.

At one time I was fascinated by the timings of the late morning trains at Erwood because they appeared to be scheduled to collide on a single line; the working book showed otherwise. The up loop is signalled for working in either direction, and the train is composed of two Great Western coaches. *2625/1911*

46527

46523
ERWOOD

1445
CYCLING
PROHIBITED

GENTLEMEN

**Caerau, West Glam; GWR '51XX' 0-6-0T No 4144, 1.30 pm Bridgend-Cymmer Afan.**
**Llangynwyd, Mid Glam; same train, both 1 June 1962.**
Again you are seeing the same train twice (with the help of the car this time). The miners' institute dominates the scene at Caerau, where the train has just entered a single line prior to a tunnel which emerges in Cymmer Afan station.

At Llangynwyd the signalman is holding the token for the single line, whilst in the foreground is the apparatus for handling it when he is not about. I believe the locomotive may be preserved; certainly someone wrote for a copy of this picture years ago when such action was intended. *2683/2682*

***Above left*** **Ludlow, Shropshire; GWR '14XX' 0-4-2T No 1445, 3.15 pm Leominster-Craven Arms & Stokesay.**
***Left*** **Tenbury Wells, Hereford & Worcs; GWR '14XX' 0-4-2T No 1445, 4.46 pm to Woofferton, both 18 April 1960.**
Here you are looking at the front and back of the same train, and its itinerary meanwhile is recorded in the text (page 154). The banner repeater at the tunnel entrance will record the position of the next signal out of sight around the corner - I love the neat fencing above the tunnel. Why the need for a specific notice banning cycling I know not.

At Tenbury Wells everyone seems to be preparing for the homeward journey at the end of the Bank Holiday. The signal box seems to be a one-off, neither GWR nor LNWR. Lighting is by gas once more; until quite recently BR must have remained one of the biggest customers for gas mantles - a clear indicator of the lack of investment! *1915/1916*

***Left*** **Farrington Gurney Halt, Avon; GWR '57XX' 0-6-0PT No 7784, 1.30 pm Bristol (Temple Meads)-Frome, 16 May 1959.**
***Below*** **Bampton, Devon; GWR '57XX' 0-6-0PT No 7761, 1.35 pm Dulverton-Exeter (St Davids), 26 February 1960.**
Two pannier tanks - and passengers in both cases! The upper loco bears the GWR branch passenger train headcode. It's a day of exploration on the North Somerset Line.

I really love the view of Bampton; it's a perfect model of a country branch-line station. Do notice the signal on the top of the cutting (left background) to facilitate sighting by the driver. The signalman is on the platform with the single line staff to Tiverton, and there are gothic windows in the down waiting room opposite. The rest of the day has been spent between Barnstaple and Taunton and on the Minehead line. *1611/1878*

***Right*** **Symonds Yat, Glos; GWR '14XX' 0-4-2T No 1445, 11.00 am Ross-on-Wye-Monmouth (Troy), 6 May 1958.**
***Below right*** **Chipping Norton, Oxon; GWR '51XX' 2-6-2T No 4109, 4.35 pm to Kingham, 4 November 1961.**
I mentioned Symonds Yat earlier (page 16) and here we are! There's a camping coach for holidays in the remains of the loop, and a public telephone is provided. It was on Whit Monday 1956 that I first called at this station by train during a circular itinerary involving changes at Southampton, Cheltenham, Gloucester, Ross-on-Wye, Monmouth, Severn Tunnel Junction and Salisbury.

I included Chipping Norton in a journey to Evesham which, if my diary is accurate, cost £2 13s 6d. *1238/2552*

SYMONDS YAT
1445

4109

***Left*** **Cassington Halt, Oxon; GWR '74XX' 0-6-0PT No 7445, 4.24 pm Oxford-Fairford, 27 March 1961.**
***Below*** **Lechlade, Glos; GWR '74XX' 0-6-0PT No 7411, 12.15 pm Oxford-Fairford, 5 July 1958.**

The Fairford branch was a favourite of mine, running as it did through the lovely Upper Thames valley. I was just returning from Bantry with Bob and Phyl Kirkland and had turned off the A40 briefly as this train was due at Cassington Halt. We had heard that the line from Cork was likely to close shortly and had made a one-day visit to Southern Ireland using cabins on the boat from Fishguard to Rosslare and back as overnight accommodation.

Lechlade was photographed during a more routine visit to the branch with Gerald Daniels and Edwin Wilmshurst which also included the DN&SR and the M&SWJR. The halt was relatively modern; the garden at Lechlade was a picture - the loop is in the goods yard. *2363/1351*

***Right*** **Burrator Halt, Devon; GWR '44XX' 2-6-2T No 4410, 11.19 am Yelverton-Princetown.**
***Below right*** **Yelverton, Devon; same train, both 6 July 1955.**

And last in this section are two of my earliest pictures before my UK itinerary began in earnest. My two friends - Neville Grabaskey and Dennis Baston - are standing by the engine driver, all enjoying the sunny morning. Little did we know the closures to come; Princetown ended the following March and Yelverton itself in 1962. *596/597*

4410

# 8. Branch line termini

In Scotland, Comrie (page 83), closed in July 1964, had become a terminus simply because the line beyond there by Loch Earn to the Callandar & Oban had closed in 1951. Only two trains ran each weekday by the time that Alan and I made our journey on 16 May 1964. We had just come up from London by Motorail and drove out to Crieff before breakfast in order to use the morning service. The coaches smelt of apples which was rather nice.

Upper Greenock Junction (where we entered the single line section to Inverkip and Wemyss Bay, page 84) is the only place at which I have witnessed token exchange by a dog. Obviously the signalman there had carried out due training and the animal kept the metal hoop, containing the pouch with the token, in its mouth well above the ground. I photographed this event in colour on 27 August 1965, but sadly the slide is underexposed.

We caused some concern to the bus conductress on the route from the rail terminus at Ballater (page 84) to Braemar on 22 May 1957. The circular tour tickets, which contained one for the journey by the bus, run by a rail-associated company, were issued from King's Cross, but stapled into a booklet labelled 'LNER'. She declined to accept this at first because, rightly, she said the company no longer existed. She was only reconciled to our honesty on reading the date the ticket bore. We then pointed out that on the return journey we would like to stay on board until the point where the road and railway came together at Cambus o' May Halt. We wished to photograph there a Ballater train which we had reason to believe might have a veteran engine, but feared we might just miss the bus on its run back to Ballater if the train ran at all late. She said that they would wait for us if necessary. The train ran punctually so all was well!

Let's look south now. Uppingham Station (page 85) remained, unbelievably, in LNWR colours until closure to passengers in 1960. You could still read a painter's date of 1921 on the wall. Where had the money gone taken in fares there all those years, which must have contained an element for redecoration?

Hemyock (page 87) was at the end of a branch so winding and slow that for some years a gas-lit coach was employed because a dynamo could not produce enough power to illuminate the carriages.

I was always relieved when I reached the terminus at Hawkhurst (page 90). This was due to the inclusion of the branch sometimes in a circular tour, also involving the Kent & East Sussex Railway, when timings (including a change of bus from Robertsbridge at Hurst Green) were close. I had to race on foot down the hill from the garage at Hawkhurst and up the other side to catch the last train.

One of the very few unpleasant incidents on our journeys occurred at Maiden Newton in Dorset (page 162) on 28 July 1957 during a bus strike. We had come from Dorchester, where, incredibly, Harry had insisted on a taxi between the two stations, and joined the second of the two coaches which made up the train to Bridport, as the front one was so crowded. (There's a picture of another train there on page 88). We were puzzled that this coach was empty until the Guard appeared and peremptorily ordered us out and into the one with the crowd. He would not relent and we had to stand all the way to the coast. Apparently the second coach had been added by some public-spirited Yard Master at Weymouth, but it ran empty as the Guard felt greater allegiance to his bus colleagues (also in the NUR) than to his customers. It was a sign of things to come.

The picture at Barnstaple (Victoria Road) was taken on Whit Monday 1960, a few days prior to closure to passengers, at the end of a holiday in Yorkshire and the Lake District, strange as that may seem. We had boarded the last train from Hellifield via Clitheroe on the Saturday night, which terminated at Bolton. There I spied an elephant on the platform amongst the contingent from Bertram Mills Circus which usually travelled by train. Then in Manchester we took a taxi to Mayfield station which was being used for sleeper traffic at that time due to the reconstruction of London Road. We awoke and got out at Taunton on the Sunday morning before making a day trip to Minehead, spending the next night at Williton, and arriving back at Norton Fitzwarren in time for the train (in the picture on page 88) to Ilfracombe. We all felt so tired later that day that we cut short our prepared itinerary and made for home!

My last comment is reserved for the terminus at Wallingford (closed to passengers in 1959) (page 89). Harry is sitting in the picture prior to a fast walk to the town centre to join a bus to Abingdon where we could pick up another train, to Radley, on 14 June 1958. Those with a sharp eye or a good memory will recognise this as the day of the change, later, at Savernake Low Level (page 10). The end of that journey proved momentous. The approach to Andover from the west consisted of the up and down main line to Salisbury and a further line on the north side often used by trains from Cheltenham. The two routes came together at Red Post Junction, and on the evening in question we were held there by a signal. Our intention was to join the last up express which we had christened the 'Pork Chop Train' because we had come to use it repeatedly from various places in the West Country. It had a friendly crew and they produced exceedingly good pork chops!

The delay therefore caused us some concern and I was

sent along the totally empty train to explain our predicament to the Guard. He immediately called up to the signalman who explained that shunting was taking place at Andover Junction. By this time the express was in sight and soon overtook us at the signal. It was, however, held in the station until we arrived, so all was well!

**Rothbury, Northumberland; NER 'J25' 0-6-0 No 65727, engine off goods from Morpeth, 26 May 1959.**
**Kirkcudbright, Dumfries & Galloway; LMS '3MT' 2-6-2T No 40151, 9.35 am to Castle Douglas, 30 May 1959.**

Two terminals, east and west near the Scottish Border, and both visited during one holiday. Between these pictures Alan and I went by train to Berwick, Wooler, Kelso, Greenlaw and Carlisle.

The engine was a tight fit on the turntable at Rothbury and needed careful handling; it was the only way to the shed and was provided with an additional bolt lock for use when set for the platform. I made some recordings during our trip which were used on the BBC 'On Railways' programme and later on Radio York. There is a favourite interview with the lady at Brinkburn having her water brought by the train. The extensive bell code used by the signalman was, I suspect, a joke, as the goods ran only twice a week and there were no other trains. The Guard's Geordie dialect was such that I needed an interpreter.

Scottish frugality is in evidence at Kirkcudbright where the Glasgow & South Western Railway signal is fixed to the wall of the engine shed. Although we stayed but one night there, the hotel sent me a Christmas card for years. *1632/1660*

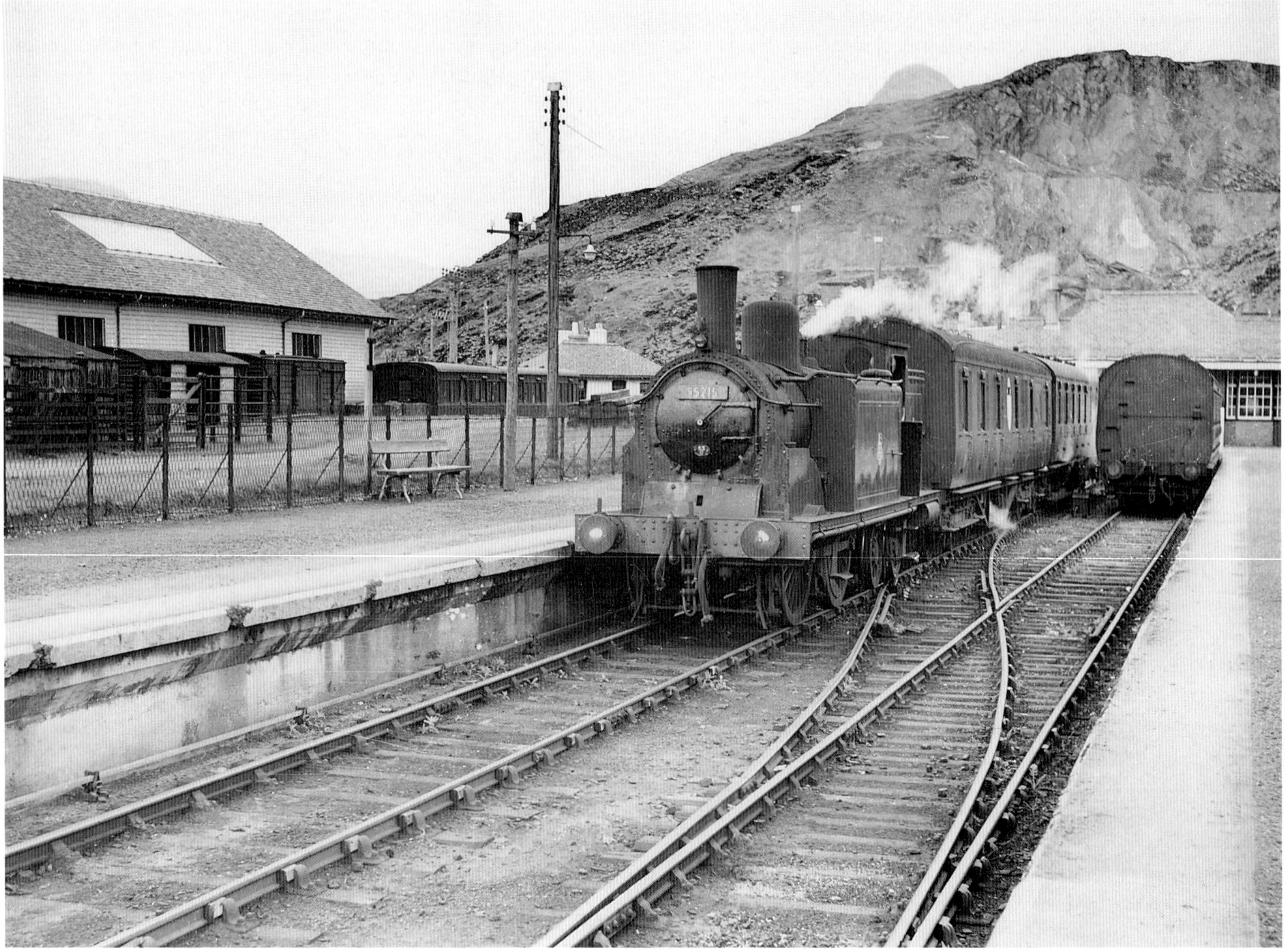

***Above*** **Ballachulish, Highland; CR '2P' 0-4-4T No 55215, 3.38 pm to Oban, 30 May 1957.**
***Left*** **Aberfeldy, Tayside; CR '2P' 0-4-4T No 55209, 10.28 am from Ballinluig, 24 May 1957.**
Similar locos (the one at Ballachulish with a stove-pipe chimney) at the ends of two Scottish branch lines. Between the pictures Alan and I had travelled by rail to Crieff, the Callandar & Oban, Fort William, Wick and Thurso, Dornoch, the Kyle of Lochalsh and Mallaig, all behind steam!

We had lunch in the refreshment room at Ballachulish and I recall the over-supply of potatoes relative to the quantity of meat. The coach at Aberfeldy is an early Stanier LMS BCK with 1st Class at the outer end and has worked through from Perth, replacing a coach going the other way, presumably for cleaning or maintenance. *1025/997*

***Above right*** **Crieff, Tayside; LMS Class '5' 4-6-0 No 45473, 7.48 am Comrie-Gleneagles.**
***Right*** **Comrie, Tayside; same locomotive, to Crieff, both 16 May 1964.**
Consecutive pictures, and referred to in the text (page 80). Looking at the awning at Crieff it seems that a section was removed every time it became unsafe, and nothing restored. No 45473 is in my pictures of Crieff in 1957, so it must have worked there for years. On this occasion it is deputising for a railbus. *3154/3155*

**Ballater, Grampian; BR '4MT' 2-6-4T No 80028, 3.18 pm from Aberdeen, 22 May 1957.**
It surprised me when the branch from Aberdeen to Ballater closed as it was used regularly by the Royal Train en route to Balmoral; the long shed in the background was there to house the vehicles. Presumably the politicians aimed to show that all levels of society were to do without trains! The story of our visit is in the text on page 80. 980

**Wemyss Bay, Strathclyde; LMS '4MT' 2-6-4T No 42265, 3.30 pm to Glasgow (Central), 23 May 1964.**
Wemyss Bay station is listed, but looks very sorry for itself today though the trains are modern. It used to be one of Scotland's best-kept stations with hanging baskets of flowers on the concourse and on the covered way to the steamers for Rothsey. *3186*

**Uppingham, Leics; LTSR '3P' 4-4-2T No 41975, 1.15 pm from Seaton. Same location, same locomotive, 12.24 pm to Seaton, both 18 July 1959.** Two more consecutive pictures and my particular favourites. I've mentioned Uppingham in the text (page 80). The first shows the Tilbury Tank and its one coach arriving from Seaton by the lofty LNWR lower quadrant signal, which also carries the outgoing arm (almost lost in the trees behind) lower down on the same post. There is a small ground-frame in the foreground.

In the second photograph the engine has run round the coach and the crew are passing the time of day on the trolley while the Guard sweeps out the dust through the open door at the end of the coach. Was it really so much more peaceful than now? The typical LNWR station is painted in that company's country colours of green and cream and the station house is in Crewe brick. *1743/1744*

NOTICE
CLOAK ROOM
5804

5804

**Opposite page** Tetbury, Glos; GWR '58XX' 0-4-2T No 5804, 3.25 pm from Kemble, becoming 3.50 pm to Kemble, both 27 December 1958.

***This page*** **Hemyock, Devon; GWR '14XX' 0-4-2T No 1468, 1.40 pm from Tiverton Junction, both 10 September 1959.**

Great Western throughout - even to the extent of an original notice on the wall at Tetbury and a blue enamel platform sign (beside an ornate gas-lamp in the lower picture), together with a loading gauge. The station closed in 1964 (after experiments with a railbus to please the then Chairman of BR who lived nearby).

It's a gorgeous afternoon at Hemyock - one feels like fishing in the stream - and Harry, Alan and I have sauntered along the Culm Valley in the gas-lit ex-Barry Railway coach. A milk tank - milk was the mainstay of the line - hides between the train and the water tower. Hemyock closed in 1963. *1470/1471; 1823/1824*

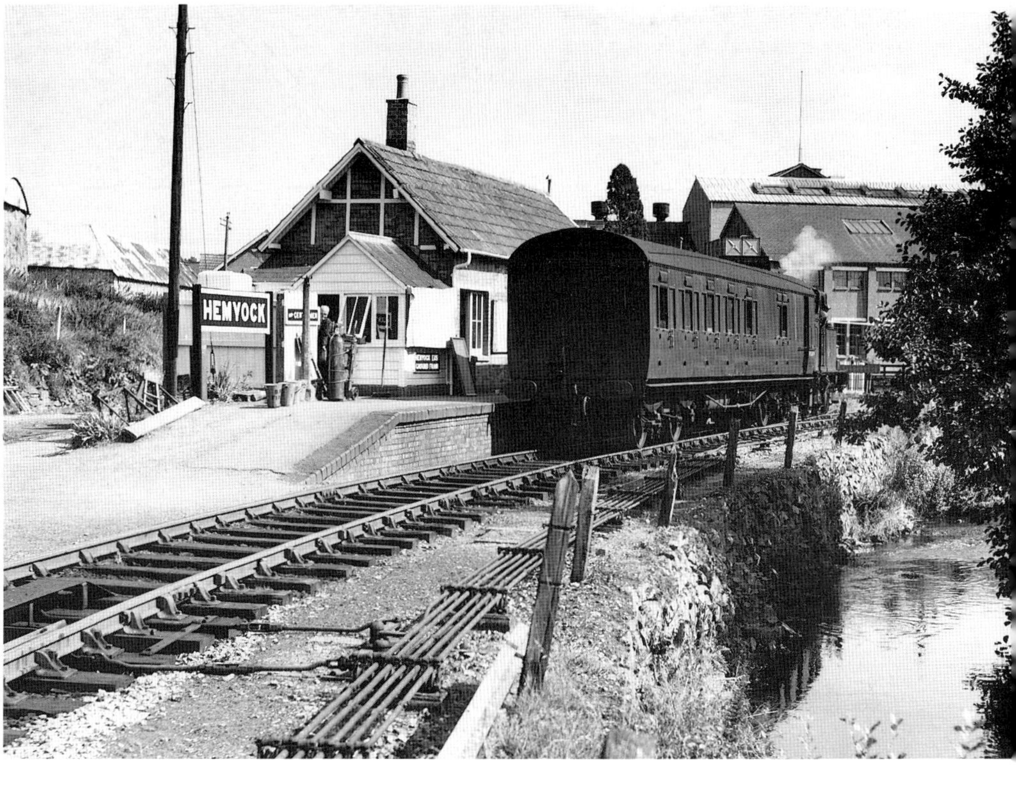

*Above* Barnstaple (Victoria Road), Devon; GWR '43XX' 2-6-0 No 6309, 10.15 am Taunton-Ilfracombe, 6 June 1960.
*Left* Bridport, Dorset; GWR '57XX' 0-6-0PT No 3746, 4.38 pm to Maiden Newton, 13 July 1957.
*Above right* Wallingford, Oxon; GWR '14XX' 0-4-2T No 1407, 4.35 pm to Cholsey & Moulsford, 14 June 1958.
*Right* Cardigan, Dyfed; GWR '4575' 2-6-2T No 5549, 5.45 pm to Whitland, 9 May 1958.
Four more Great Western termini! Why Victoria Road, a poorly sited station for Barnstaple, survived until 1960 I fail to understand. Only then were all the Taunton trains diverted to Barnstaple Junction with obvious links to the Southern services. Our mammoth journey from the north is described in the text on page 80. Similarly our experiences to and from Bridport and Wallingford, where Harry is sitting in the sun. Rain is the order of the day at Cardigan, where the pile of parcels should have augured well for the future of branch. Closures took place in all cases, in 1960, 1975, 1959 and 1962 respectively - what a waste of resources! *2053/1046/1325/1264*

1407
GENTLEMEN
WALLINGFORD

CARDIGAN
GENTLEMEN
5549

***Above*** **Allhallows-on-Sea, Kent; SECR 'H' 0-4-4T No 31512, 11.29 am to Gravesend, 15 September 1957.**
***Left*** **Hawkhurst, Kent; unidentified SECR 'H' 0-4-4T, 6.35 pm to Paddock Wood, 21 August 1957.**
***Above right*** **Swanage, Dorset; LSWR 'M7' 0-4-4T No 30052, 2.25 pm to Wareham, 19 May 1963.**
***Right*** **Lyme Regis, Dorset; LSWR '0415' 4-4-2T No 30582, 12.33 pm from Axminster, 22 August 1957.**

Let's finish this section on the Southern Railway, three of the pictures being taken in 1957.

The company had hoped to develop Allhallows as a resort to compete with Southend across the water but, like Ravenscar in the north, natural factors intervened - cold winds off the east coast and mud, rather than sand. The circular tour involving Allhallows shows how much could be covered in a day without effort. We used the 10.42 from Gravesend and 11.29 return, then 12.28 to Chatham, 1.31 to Sittingbourne, 2.10 to Sheerness and 3 pm return, 3.49 to Faversham, 4.08 to Dover, 5.30 to Folkestone, 6.00 to Sevenoaks, 7.33 to Dunton Green, 7.50 to Westerham and 8.23 return, and finally the 8.36 back to London.

Space precludes details of the trips to the other terminals, except to say that the Hawkhurst branch ended well outside the town, with a strenuous walk down and up hill to reach the station (see page 80). Swanage has been revived, Lyme Regis has gone. Closures took effect at all locations in 1961 (2), 1972 and 1965 respectively. *1093/1074/2882/1075*

30057

OUT
PARCELS &
CLOAKROOM
30582

# 9. Freight trains

I have so many stories to tell about journeys by freight train that I hardly know where to begin. And because there are so many I must be brief.

Let's start in Wales, and in the Marches. Alan and I travelled from Kington to Presteign (page 95) and back on 7 May 1958 in company with an Inspector who had come all the way from Chester to be with us. This involved him coming south to Leominster and joining the freight there. He explained that he would not be home until very late because his connection would pass across the junction at Leominster while the returning freight was waiting to gain access to the main line. We were in the car that day and our next night was to be spent in Carmarthen. So he thumbed a lift from us, as it were, to Hay on Wye, where he could take an earlier train to Hereford and see the freight as he tore through Leominster.

At Pontrhythallt (page 101) on the Llanberis branch on 22 May 1962 a lot of time was spent loading a double bed into one of the vans.

You may recall that we travelled to the Hope exchange station from Ruthin (page 24). To get there we had arranged to use the freight train from Corwen (seen in the picture of Nantclwyd on page 100). This was operated by the London Midland Region from a station in the Western Region. We duly produced our brake-van permits (see page 7) to the booking office clerk in order to purchase travel tickets, only to be told that they were nothing to do with him. He did, however, authorise us to go into the goods yard, so all was well - but we never paid any fares! Although that was the only train on the branch that day and had lots of time to spare, nevertheless another locomotive and crew were passed at Gwyddelwern on ballast duties, necessitating the employment of a signalman there to cross the trains.

When we went to Coniston (pictures at Broughton and Woodland on page 103 and Torver on page 177) we expected to join the goods at Foxfield, but the LMR instructed us to go instead to Kirkby in Furness (page 159). We arrived there from Millom on 1 June 1960 and sought the usual tickets to accompany the permits. Again the booking clerk denied all knowledge but rang the signalman to put the signals against the goods so that it would stop and we could get on board. There were more staff in the brake-van that day than I was to see on any other trip - it was packed - and Harry couldn't refrain from asking what everyone was doing. Signalling duties at Coniston was the reply. As the crossovers were changed by hand for the loco to run round the wagons, and there appeared to be only one operative lever in the signal box, we came to the conclusion that, like us, the staff were enjoying a day out in the sunshine. The branch closed two years later.

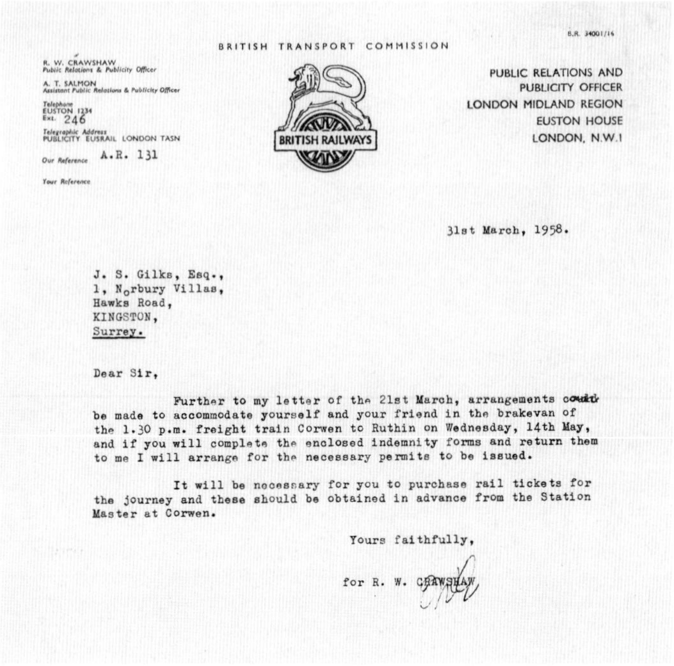

B.R. 34001/16

BRITISH TRANSPORT COMMISSION

R. W. CRAWSHAW
*Public Relations & Publicity Officer*
A. T. SALMON
*Assistant Public Relations & Publicity Officer*
Telephone
EUSTON 1234
Ext. 246
Telegraphic Address
PUBLICITY EUSRAIL LONDON TASN
Our Reference A.R. 131
Your Reference

BRITISH RAILWAYS

PUBLIC RELATIONS AND
PUBLICITY OFFICER
LONDON MIDLAND REGION
EUSTON HOUSE
LONDON, N.W.1

31st March, 1958.

J. S. Gilks, Esq.,
1, Norbury Villas,
Hawks Road,
KINGSTON,
Surrey.

Dear Sir,

Further to my letter of the 21st March, arrangements could be made to accommodate yourself and your friend in the brakevan of the 1.30 p.m. freight train Corwen to Ruthin on Wednesday, 14th May, and if you will complete the enclosed indemnity forms and return them to me I will arrange for the necessary permits to be issued.

It will be necessary for you to purchase rail tickets for the journey and these should be obtained in advance from the Station Master at Corwen.

Yours faithfully,

for R. W. CRAWSHAW

Nearby, at Haverthwaite (page 102), now the Lakeside Railway, the previous day the Guard had advised us that the engine driver did not wish to take us to Lakeside. I managed to persuade him to ring Control about this, as we had travelled all the way from the south to make the trip. That had the desired effect, but the driver was not amused, drove us very fast over the rough track and barely gave us time to photograph the loco at Lakeside.

The train at Kineton (page 105), on a Sunday, reminds me of the apparent folly of BR in the Beeching era, or so it seemed to me from outside the industry. Much of the Stratford-on-Avon & Midland Junction Railway had just been relaid with heavier rail and firmer ballast to accommodate heavy trains of iron ore from the South Midlands to South Wales. I saw chairs dated 1963 just east of Fenny Compton, yet within two years the track there was taken up again. Surely, having been modernised, it was worth employing the infrastructure for a while rather than dismantling it so soon?

On the Grassington branch freight (page 104) on 25 May 1960 I was cross-examined by the Guard as to my trade union allegiance. He seemed satisfied when, as a local government officer, I explained that I was a member of NALGO (now Unison).

The freight to Wooler via Kelso on 28 May 1959 (illustrated at Coldstream on page 114) was run on a bonus-ticket system. As I understand it, this meant that the quicker the turn could be completed the more money was due to the crew. Bearing this in mind, we were anxious to be extra punctual at Tweedmouth yard at 7.30 am and were in the bus garage in Berwick for the 7.10 across the bridge. When this failed to appear we were really alarmed. Into the depot I went, to be informed that the service was cancelled, but that, in the circumstances, a fitter would drive a bus across for us, and this he duly did! The freight trip was carried out at incredible speed, and the Guard barely had time to close the level crossing gates at Hagg, for instance, before we were under way again. Since the introduction of bonus-ticket working, he told us, the train had already slipped back there on wet greasy rails and smashed the gates on two occasions. So much for practice versus theory in the world of economics.

The picture at Duns (page 113) reminds me that on Bank Holiday Mondays in England the freight, usually steam-hauled from Tweedmouth, was diesel-hauled from north of the Border.

The train facing the camera at Jervaulx (page 109) had, unbeknown to us on the pick-up goods to Hawes, set fire to a telegraph pole at Constable Burton which in turn had broken the communication with Leyburn. Accordingly we had to wait whilst a pilotman drove from Leyburn to guarantee that the single line ahead was clear for us to use. This created delay and there was talk among the staff of aborting the trip. I had to convince everyone of our need to reach Hawes, which was duly perceived, and ring the taximan there who was to take us to Garsdale. Although we were very late getting there, fortunately the train from Settle to Carlisle was equally late and we made our connection.

Friday 29 May 1964 was an interesting day. We had permits to travel by the freight from Galashiels to Selkirk at around 9.00 am, then from Kelso to Jedburgh (page 115) and back later that morning. We were chided by the guard at Galashiels for being late, whereas according to our letter from HQ we were half-an-hour early. On arrival at Selkirk we hurried out of the station to catch the only bus of the day which passed that way - just right for us - and were soon back in Galashiels and in the car to Kelso. Here, to our amazement, we were confronted by the 'Jubilee' locomotive *Arethusa*, attached, boiler first, to just a brake-van. We were whirled to Roxburgh and down the branch, stopping at Kirkbank to deliver water supplies to the old couple who occupied the crossing-keeper's cottage. I was told off by the gate-keeper for helping him open the gates - they no longer had hinges - as the effort was good for his arthritis!

Ravenswood Junction (page 118) brings back memories of a freight trip to Greenlaw five years earlier to the very day. After the return trip from St Boswells we intended to travel south to Carlisle. On hearing this the guard asked whether we would like to use the 'Waverley' express. We had assumed we would be too late for this and had planned to take a later train. He said, however, that he would arrange for the goods to precede it on our return to Ravenswood Junction. Sure enough, there stood the London express held at the junction signal while we sailed out on to the main line in our brake-van. A sprint across the yard at St Boswells and we were into the express. We got out again at Hawick, the next stop, for the extra time gave us an opportunity to see the town.

The ongoing train has memories too. It was virtually empty and the Guard invited us to take seats in a 1st Class compartment so we could go to sleep. Nothing was farther from my mind through that magnificent scenery, but it was nice to be pampered. At Riccarton Junction, then still cut off from any recognised road, I saw from the carriage window a man having a tooth extracted in the waiting room - by a dentist I hasten to add. It was the practice to use the place as a consulting room.

The journey from Forfar to Careston (page 120) had to be on a Tuesday because the train only ran on that day; there were no other trains during the week. We joined it on 19 May 1964 and were surprised when, at Justinhaugh, the loco ran round the wagons and we were propelled the last six miles, no one looking ahead out of the brake-van except ourselves! The train was scheduled to remain at the rural outpost - nothing there but The Mains of Careston - for nearly three hours, and the Guard said that the crew would be playing cards; what would we like to do? We explained that a taxi was coming (about an hour later) to take us to another freight in Brechin. Careston was so quiet that we could hear and see the taxi long before it turned up. The driver insisted on showing us Brechin Cathedral (inside) before taking us to the station.

There stood the freight seen in the picture at Edzell (page 120). The Guard explained that there was no traffic for the branch, nor any to bring back, but that the crew had assembled some trucks to justify our trip. They would be happy to stop for photographs on the way back when the sun was in the right position - and they did. Later we returned with them to Montrose, necessitating reversal at the famous Kinnaber Junction and propelling along the up East Coast Main Line for three miles.

When we travelled with the freight down the Isle of Whithorn (illustrations at Wigtown and Sorbie on page 117) we stressed that we would like to go to Garlieston as well as Whithorn itself. The service ran only on Tuesday and Thursday and there were no other trains; evidently none had been to Garlieston for some time. Naturally the signalman at Mill Isle Junction set the route for Whithorn and the guard had to walk to his box, the train set back and the signals adjusted to allow us to traverse the Garlieston branch. No wonder they hesitated to go down there. Just outside the town was a five cross road without level crossing gates. The guard had his hands full trying to stop the road traffic.

My last freight story concerns our journey from Macduff on the Buchan coast (illustrations at Rothie Norman, Wartle and Inveramsey on pages 121 and 122) on Monday 1 June 1959. I wrote my usual letter for two brake-van permits to the Divisional Manager at

Aberdeen and was surprised when these were abruptly refused. I tried again, pointing out that there must be some mistake as the Working Timetable clearly showed the public were in fact allowed to use this train on payment of 1st Class fare (there were a few such cases). Again a peremptory refusal. So I had to go over the head of one S. E. (later Sir Stanley) Raymond, who was to become Chairman of BR and to be sacked by Mrs Barbara Castle (perhaps because her experiences in dealing with him were similar to mine), and get the permit from our old friend Cyril Rider, PRO of the Western.

Had Mr Raymond travelled on the train he might have realised how badly this aspect of his district was managed. The train was scheduled to leave Macduff at 8.25 am (having left Aberdeen in the early hours for some reason lost in obscurity), but we had heard that it had a habit of going before 6 o'clock! Having got the permits, I asked Mr Raymond to ensure that it did not leave early as we wanted breakfast at a reasonable hour in our hotel. It was standing in the yard when we arrived and left exactly on time. To our surprise, at Turriff another crew appeared and the first took the bus back to Aberdeen. We then spent the morning dawdling from one station to the next for photographs. The new crew could not have been nicer. We still reached Inverurie some three hours ahead of schedule and were given a tour of the railway works. What a way to run a railway! But how enjoyable for us.

***Below*** **Longville, Shropshire; GWR '57XX' 0-6-0PT No 4605, freight from Much Wenlock, 3 July 1956.**
In June 1956, having had some severe criticism from Charles Clinker for inaccuracies in my first (two-month) article in The Railway Magazine, I attended a course in which he participated at Attingham Hall, Shrewsbury, to learn better, and sat with him at dinner. Then I went on to spend nearly a fortnight at one of my first B&Bs in All Stretton. It was very nice but illustrates how times have changed, for the owner brought hot water in a jug to fill a basin in the bedroom for washing each morning! I failed to photograph Marsh Farm Junction at the time and never had another opportunity before it was dismantled - a lesson learned for the future - but did catch the goods at Longville in the Dale, below Wenlock Edge, on its run from Much Wenlock and back. Later I rode it and found that while normally it brought only a brake-van to Longville, on the return journey it picked up empty wagons at Presthope, presumably for the breaker's yard. *819*

***Right*** **Titley Junction, Hereford & Worcs; GWR '57XX' 0-6-0PT No 9717, Kington-Presteign freight**
***Below right*** **Presteign, Powys; same locomotive, freight from Kington, both 7 May 1958.**
Further south the freight was still running between Kington and Presteign as an extension of its trip from Leominster (and from time to time to Dolyhir as well). I mention this in the text (page 92). Note that the signal at Titley Junction boasts a route indicator! Note also the pole carried by the shunter at the terminus. Two years earlier I had visited the branch by car and called at Forge Crossing Halt. Here the crossing-keeper, an old lady who told me she was over ninety, warned me of the possible approach of the goods. She lived in the adjacent cottage and was very conscientious. *1251/1252*

9717

TELEPHONE
9717

***Above*** **Near Torpantau Tunnel (north portal), Powys; GWR '57XX' 0-6-0PT No 4632 banked by '57XX' No 9643, Brecon-Merthyr Tydfil freight, 20 August 1959.**

***Left*** **Near Merthyr Tydfil, Mid Glam; unidentified GWR '57XX' 0-6-0PTs, Brecon-Merthyr Tydfil freight, 24 March 1961.**

The goods from Brecon to Merthyr Tydfil had to climb up and over the Brecon Beacons through Torpantau (see page 62, and note its fixed distant signal) and diverged from the route to Newport at Pontsticill Junction. The first picture on the 1 in 27 gradient does not disclose the banker which is out of sight round the bend but working hard as the front loco approaches the tunnel mouth to my left. The second picture, eighteen months later, shows the train nearing its destination. Like the photo at Horspath Halt (page 23), unusually the back of the train is shown. *1790/2348*

***Above right*** **Glascoed Halt, Gwent; unidentified GWR '57XX' 0-6-0PT, freight from Pontypool Road, 23 March 1961.**

***Right*** **Hengoed (Low Level), Mid Glam; GWR '56XX' 0-6-2T No 6635, northbound freight, 18 May 1961.**

Glascoed Halt had been closed for nearly six years, but work was still in progress on track removal when this train was being backed into the ordnance depot. The line to Monmouth left the Hereford/Newport route at Little Mill Junction near Pontypool Road.

The two-tier station at Hengoed was one of several of its design and is mentioned in the text (page 24). I've just alighted upstairs from a train from Quaker's Yard where again I had changed from the Low Level station on the Cardiff/Merthyr route to the High Level on the east/west Neath to Pontypool Road. Now I'm going to Cardiff. *2337/2413*

RAILWAY
BRIDGE
WAY OUT
AND TO
HIGH LEVEL STN
6635
H
06
HENGOED
(LOW LEVEL)

**Felin Fach, Dyfed; GWR '74XX' 0-6-0PT No 7444, Lampeter-Aberayron freight, 10 May 1958.**
When Harry, Alan and myself went to Lampeter in my Morris Minor we found the Guard of our train to Aberayron pacing the approach road impatient for our arrival. According to the papers sent to me we were in good time, but again local conditions were different on a Saturday morning. The eastbound train was made up of vans, but as you can see we went out on a mixed freight. Felin Fach was to prove the terminus in 1970 of passengers from Surbiton by a private DMU in connection with my charter of the Blue Pullman to Carmarthen. Little did I expect such developments in 1958! *1268*

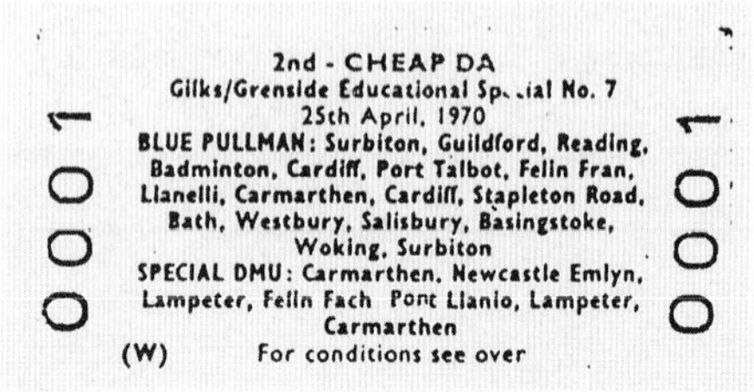
0001
2nd - CHEAP DA
Gilks/Grenside Educational Sp.ial No. 7
25th April, 1970
BLUE PULLMAN: Surbiton, Guildford, Reading, Badminton, Cardiff, Port Talbot, Felin Fran, Llanelli, Carmarthen, Cardiff, Stapleton Road, Bath, Westbury, Salisbury, Basingstoke, Woking, Surbiton
SPECIAL DMU: Carmarthen, Newcastle Emlyn, Lampeter, Felin Fach Pont Llanio, Lampeter, Carmarthen
(W) For conditions see over
0001

**Glyncorrwg, West Glam; unidentified GWR '57XX' 0-6-0PT, miners' train from North Rhondda Colliery, 24 March 1961.**
I'm with Bob and Phyl Kirkland in the Rhondda. He was most anxious to see this train composed, as it is, of ex-London Division stock suitable for working over the Metropolitan Line underground between Paddington and Moorgate. Perhaps it felt at home bringing miners back from the pit! *2350*

**Cwm Prysor, Gwynedd; GWR '57XX' 0-6-0PT No 4617, Bala-Blaenau Ffestiniog freight, 13 May 1958.**
**Trevor, Clwyd; GWR '16XX' 0-6-0PT No 1628, Llangollen-Croes Newydd freight, 4 June 1965.**
On the Ruabon/Barmouth and associated Blaenau line. Having ridden the goods on the branch the previous day, Alan and I now returned in the car to see it recovering from a 15 mph temporary speed restriction on the bank.

It was Ian and I who saw the other goods in the Vale of Llangollen and caught up with its again at Trevor. Later that day I inadvertently offended him and he didn't speak with me for 19 hours - what wonderful self-discipline! *1285/3458*

**Chwilog, Gwynedd; LMS '4MT' 2-6-4T No 42601, Afonwen-Bangor freight, 22 May 1962.**
**Nantclwyd, Clwyd; LMS '2MT' 2-6-0 No 46433, Corwen-Ruthin freight, 14 May 1958.**
Two ex-LMS lines in North Wales. The closure of the first, from Afon Wen, between Portmadoc and Pwllheli, to Caernarvon & Menai Bridge near Bangor, robbed passengers of a circular cruise by rail (and the Welsh, with the Carmarthen/Aberystwyth, of an internal through route), and was short-sighted. There were weekly excursion trains in the summer which used this line and the other that is featured, from Rhyl to Corwen, as a superb tour. I comment in the text about the latter journey (page 92). *2651/1290*

**Bethesda, Gwynedd; BR '2MT' 2-6-0 No 78059, freight from Bangor, 23 May 1962.**
**Pontrhythallt, Gwynedd; LMS '4F' 0-6-0 No 44504, Bangor-Llanberis freight, 22 May 1962.**
In order to include the Bethesda and Llanberis branches in our UK itinerary, brake-van permits were obtained and Alan and I took up residence at the Menai Bridge Hotel. Harry travelled from London on Sunday night, using the sleeper to Holyhead and returning to Bangor on the first express, having breakfast on the way - thus he transferred from dining-car to brake-van! The junction for Bethesda was adjacent to the end of the tunnel immediately east of Bangor station and its signals were often obscured by smoke.

After travelling to and from Llanberis we would have the afternoon to spare. How nice it would be to take the train to Portmadoc, but if we did so we could not get back to the hotel in time for dinner. I noticed that road and rail from Caernarvon part company at Brynkir and that the A4085 (now A499) heads direct to Portmadoc. There happened to be a northbound bus along here from Portmadoc which would just connect with an earlier train to Menai Bridge at Brynkir station if everyone concerned was aware of our interest. So we called at Brynkir station the previous day, explained the situation to the porter, and the connection (and dinner!) was achieved! Do notice the LNWR hand-crane at Bethesda and the LNER brake-van on the Llanberis train. *2630/2642*

58287

*Above left* Arnside, Cumbria; LMS Class '5' 4-6-0 No 45275, southbound freight, 18 May 1967.
*Left* Haverthwaite, Cumbria; MR '2F' 0-6-0 No 58287, Barrow-in-Furness-Lakeside freight, 31 May 1960.
*Above* Broughton-in-Furness, Cumbria; LMS '3F' 0-6-0 No 47317, Barrow-in-Furness-Coniston freight.
*Right* Woodland, Cumbria; same train, both 1 June 1960.

We've moved north to the Furness lines now; indeed, three of the pictures were taken on consecutive days in 1960.

Not so the first, which was taken on a visit with John and Charlotte King. Please observe the Furness Railway signal box and seats with squirrels and grapes in the ironwork. The branch to Hincaster Junction (West Coast Main Line) on the right used to carry heavy freight from Teesside (page 110), but in later years just a fortnightly passenger conveying miners to and from a convalescent home near Ulverston.

I talk about the other pictures in the text (page 92). Harry can be seen studying the old engine at Haverthwaite, now home of the preserved Lakeside Railway. He is also at Broughton in Furness with washing billowing hard nearby.
*3643/2021/2025/2026*

***Above*** **Spencer's Siding, Swinden, North Yorks; LMS '4F' 0-6-0 No 44468, Skipton-Grassington freight.**
***Left*** **Grassington, North Yorks; same locomotive, shunting freight from Skipton, both 25 May 1960.**
When I rode the goods, with Alan, to Grassington I was using my first reel of colour film and relied on my new camera with its built-in meter to quote exposures. Sadly, it was faulty, so only about one out of the 36 pictures was any use. Fortunately, as you can see, I also took black and white. Naturally I was curious to visit Spencer's Siding, as it was called at that time; today it is known as Swinden. There was a vast array of Midland signals at Grassington and these looked great in the morning sunshine. I also refer to this trip in the text (page 92). The locomotive has a tender cab. *1965/1962*

***Right*** **Kineton, Warks; WD '8F' 2-8-0 No 90218, South Wales-Woodford Halse freight, 24 July 1960.**
We were also together, with Phyl, when this picture was taken. During the day every station and junction on the Stratford-on-Avon & Midland Junction line had been photographed, and we were now making our way home. Indeed, we didn't reach there until after midnight for we lingered over a wonderful dinner, taken above the mill race at a hotel in Shipston on Stour. The picture shows two LNWR signals installed by the LMS and one GWR replacement. The sidings look busy. More information in the text (page 92). *2132*

*Above* **Duke's Drive Viaduct, Buxton, Derbys; unidentified LMS '4F' 0-6-0, northbound freight, 6 May 1961.**
Trains from Hindlow still pass over this viaduct, but not since 1954 have regular passenger trains run this way from Buxton to Ashbourne; part of the line is now the Tissington Trail of the National Park Authority. I was staying with Bob Kirkland at Hoar Cross for two nights, and explored railways in Derbyshire and Staffordshire by car. *2400*

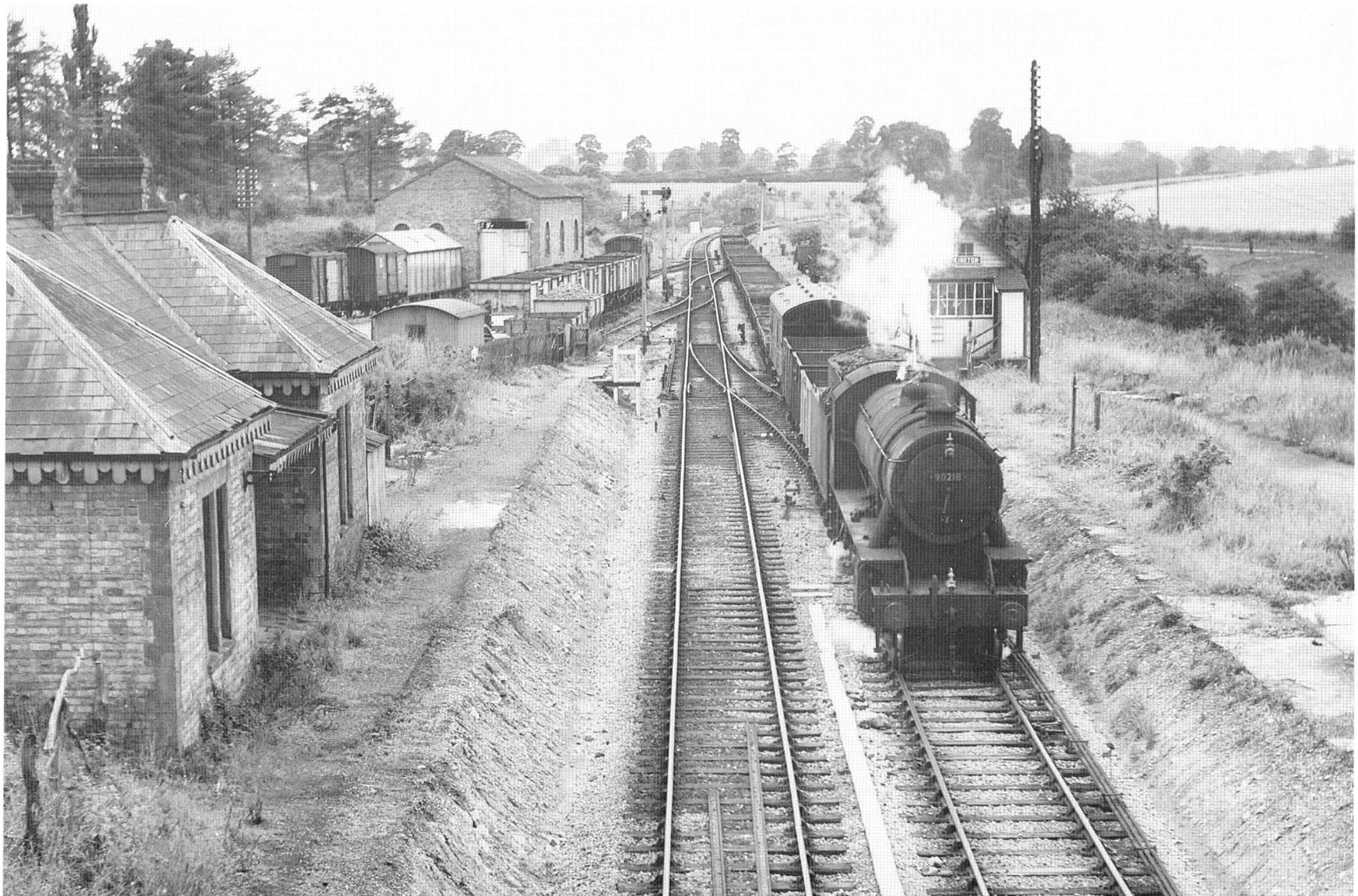

**Gretton, Northants; LMS '8F' 2-8-0 No 48387, southbound freight, 9 April 1960.**
**Scalford, Leics: LMS '8F' 2-8-0 No 48360, iron ore empties to Waltham-on-the-Wolds, 4 April 1959.**
Two Stanier Class '8' locomotives. The lines survive at Gretton, linking Corby with Manton (our cover picture), and provide a diversionary route avoiding Leicester; those at Scalford ceased to function in 1964.

There used to be a short working from Kettering to Gretton and back in the late afternoon. It was quite easy to misread the small print of Bradshaw and assume that this went to Manton and made connection there; it just so happened that an Ely-Birmingham called at Manton at about the right time and the Station Master told me he often had to calm passengers who couldn't get to Gretton that night without a taxi!

At Scalford the locomotive is running round the train preparatory to taking the branch to Wycombe Junction and Waltham-in-the-Wolds. A handsome signal box controls at least one somersault signal (right background). *1901/1550*

**Fledborough, Notts; WD '8F' 2-8-0 No 90393, westbound freight, 11 August 1962.**
**Dullingham, Cambs; GER 'J19' 0-6-0 No 64661, westbound freight, 11 October 1958.**
The link between these pictures is that the locations were both in the Eastern Region - and both survive! I used to assume that the station by High Marnham Power Station was similarly named, but discovered, after a call from Anthony Lambert, that really it was Fledborough. This train has just crossed the Trent on its way from Lincoln.

Dullingham is between Newmarket and Cambridge. Do notice the step ladders by the lamp-posts on the left to assist cleaning and insertion of the oil lamps. The posters invite us to visit Leamington Spa and North Wales. The signalman has his eye on me! *2726/1437*

***Left*** **Approaching Bishop's Stortford, Herts; unidentified GER 'J17' 0-6-0, freight from Braintree, 28 April 1956.**

***Below*** **Takeley, Essex; GER 'J17' 0-6-0 No 65545, Bishop's Stortford-Braintree freight, 22 March 1958.**

One of my first brake-van trips, passing over the old A11 road from which I had seen the bridge many times in coaches on weekend passes during National Service, but had never seen a train. My diary records that the journey was 'very nice and hilly all the way'. I recall that the loco crawled up the hills and tore down the other side.

I returned in the car two years later, having crossed London which I loathed doing, with Gerald Daniels and Edwin Wilmshurst, and also visited the Colne Valley and associated routes. I'm puzzled that the Great Eastern signal at Takeley can be cleared when the goods is passing through the loop the other way, having come along a single line. *762/1188*

***Right*** **Buntingford, Herts; LNER 'N7' 0-6-2T No 69688, shunting, 10 January 1959.**

Not far away is Buntingford (closed 1964/5). The loco has come off the passenger stock, seen in the platform, and is making up the freight train. Do notice the loading gauge by the cattle dock on the left. Beyond the signal box is a substantial water tank for replenishing locomotive boilers before venturing to St Margaret's or beyond. *1474*

*Below* **Jervaulx, North Yorks; LNER 'K1' 2-6-0 No 62003, Redmire-Northallerton limestone, and unidentified loco, Northallerton-Hawes pick-up freight, 27 May 1960.**

I talk about the events at Jervaulx in the text (page 93). The station was so named to avoid confusion, being sited in Newton-le-Willows, as on Merseyside. Daggons Road was so called for similar reasons (page 50). *1990*

**Barnard Castle, Co Durham; BR '3MT' 2-6-0 No 77003 and BR '4MT' 2-6-0 No 76049, Barrow-in-Furness-West Auckland coke empties, 4 June 1960.**

**Near Pelton, Co Durham; BR '9F' 2-10-0 No 92065 banked by Class '40' diesel-electric, Tyne Dock-Consett iron ore, 13 April 1965.**

Harry, Alan and I are waiting at Barnard Castle, having stayed overnight at Middleton-in-Teesdale, to travel direct to Tebay aboard the brake-van at the rear of the equivalent westbound working. Durham coke was particularly suitable for steel-making with haematite ore, and trains passed regularly from west Durham to Barrow-in-Furness. But not today. We have just been informed that our working had been cancelled, so our substitute plan came into action, namely by passenger train to Appleby and bus from there to Tebay. As a result I never travelled between Kirkby Stephen and Tebay by train! Do notice the NER bracket signals. Avid readers will realise that later the same day (after lunch in Tebay when I excelled myself by dropping a fried egg on to my trousers - lucky I had a change of clothes with me!) we travelled to Carnforth, changed at Wennington and soon began the overnight journey to Taunton (page 80).

A Class '40' diesel has crept into my book (not that I mind) at the rear of the iron ore wagons bound for Consett. They have doors that are air-operated from pumps sited on the right-hand side of the locomotive. *2051/3401*

**Kirkbymoorside, North Yorks; LNER 'J39' 0-6-0 No 64928, 8.50 am freight from Malton.**
**Gilling, North Yorks; same train, both 26 May 1960.**
Little did I know when I took these pictures that I would actually be living along the Gilling-Pickering line a few years later. And aren't I glad! I describe the journey in the text (page 172). The train is in a characteristic NER position at Kirkbymoorside, having shunted the wagons up hill so that they can be emptied easily into the coal merchant's lorry standing below. At Gilling the engine has run round the wagons from Malton, and the Guard is coupling up again while the driver and fireman look on. *1985/1978*

**Steel siding near Reedsmouth, Northumberland; NER 'J25' 0-6-0 No 65727, Morpeth-Bellingham freight.**
**Woodburn, Northumberland; same train, both 27 May 1959.**
Further north, two views on the Wansbeck Valley line. The remote siding to the Vickers ammunition depot (Alan and I had to hide in the brake-van while going down there!) is protected by catch-points and a gate. Note the shunter's pole.

The signal box at Woodburn is somewhat unusual; I have a colour picture of the Chairman of the local Rotary Club addressing the throng from its balcony on the day of the last special passenger train. There is a BR lorry in the yard behind the loco in crimson and cream colours. *1637/1635*

**Rothbury, Northumberland; NER 'J27' 0-6-0 No 65878, freight to Morpeth, 19 July 1963.** The goods is just setting off from Rothbury back to Scots Gap, Morpeth and on to the Blyth & Tyne. Note the North British signals. *2929*

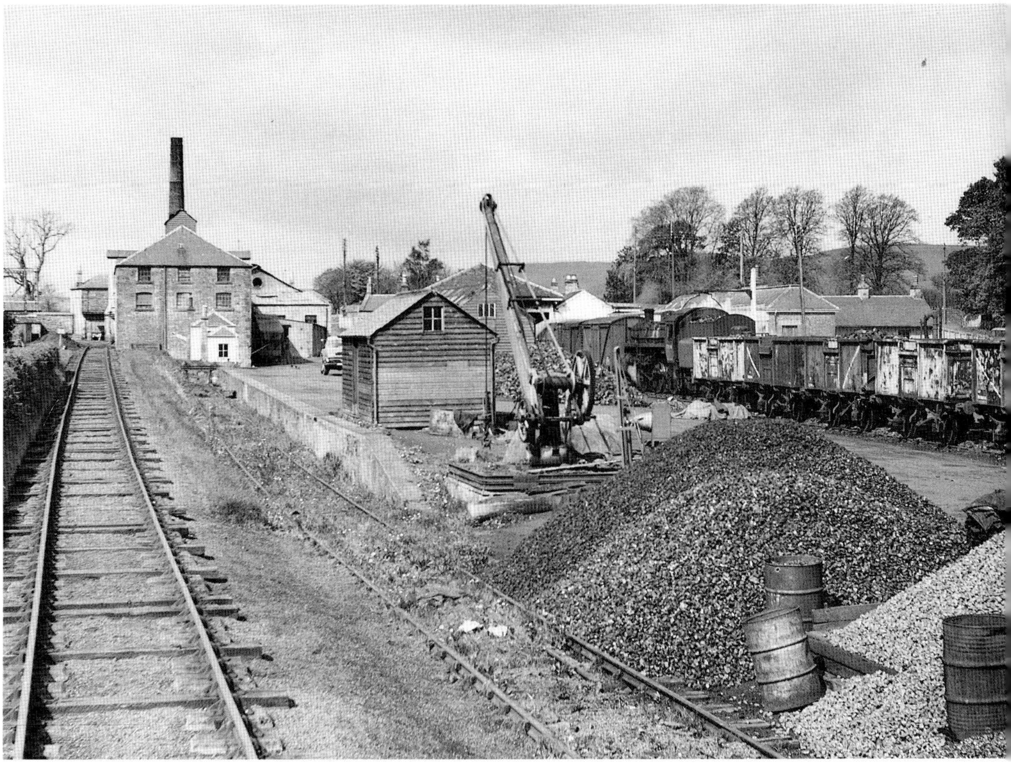

**Duns, Borders; BR '3MT' 2-6-0 No 77004, freight from Tweedmouth, 20 May 1966.** Because the freight left Tweedmouth for Duns quite early in the day I arranged to garage my car at Reston overnight and for a friend from Berwick to take Alan and myself to our hotel in Duns. There we could get only high tea, not dinner! On our return we drove from Reston to North Berwick, took the train to Corstorphine and back and finished the day in Stirling. The picture illustrates a typical branch-line terminal yard complete with fixed hand-crane. *3583*

**Coldstream, Northumberland; LMS '2MT' 2-6-0 No 46476, Tweedmouth-Wooler freight, 28 May 1959.**
**Near Maxton, Borders; LMS '6P' 4-6-0 No 45696 *Arethusa*, Jedburgh/Kelso-St Boswells freight, 29 May 1964.**
Two pictures taken about 18 miles apart on the line from Tweedmouth to St Boswells. In the first picture, more correctly at Cornhill in England, the locomotive is running round the wagons it has brought from Kelso, prior to going to Wooler. The stories behind both views are contained in my narrative (page 93). The 'Jubilee' is making good progress back to the main line. *1645/3222*

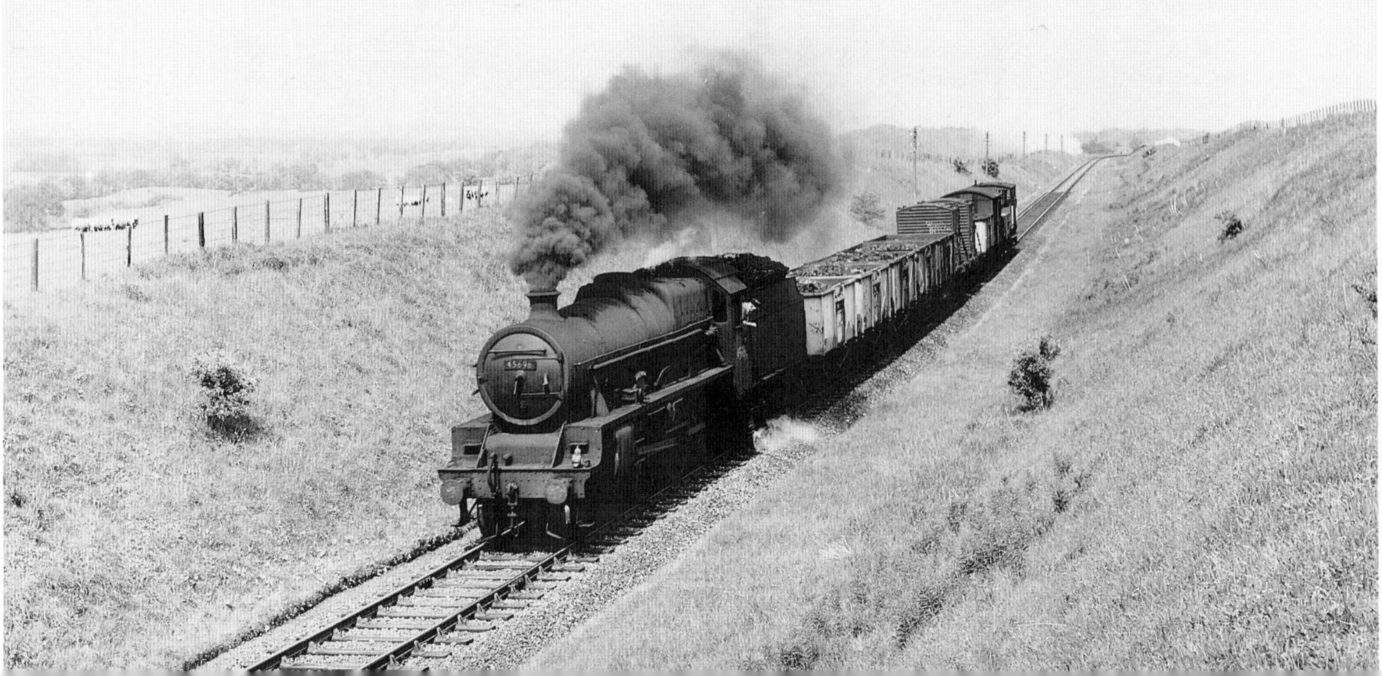

**Nisbet, Borders; LMS '6P' 4-6-0 No 45696 *Arethusa*, Jedburgh-St Boswells freight.**
**Jedburgh, Borders; same train, both 29 May 1964.**
As it's so unusual to see a 'Jubilee' on this duty, possibly the only time (?), let's look more at the Jedburgh branch, the last regular passenger train on which ran in 1948, goods in 1964. The signals at Nisbet are extraordinary, too - I've left the brake-van and nipped down into the field to capture them. The home is lower quadrant, the distant upper quadrant - it's fortunate they are well separated on the post. In practice I don't think either was worked at all!

Look at the NB signal at the terminal platform at Jedburgh, the old barrows and even the Regent (rather than Texaco) petrol station sign outside the yard. *3220/3217*

45477

44939

***Above left*** **New Galloway, Dumfries & Galloway; LMS Class '5' 4-6-0 No 45477, Stranraer-Carlisle freight, 28 May 1964.**
***Left*** **Creetown, Dumfries & Galloway; LMS Class '5' 4-6-0 No 44939, Stranraer-Dumfries freight, 27 May 1964.**
***Above*** **Wigtown, Dumfries & Galloway; LMS '2MT' 2-6-0 No 46467, Newton Stewart-Whithorn freight, 22 July 1963.**
***Right*** **Sorbie, Dumfries & Galloway; BR '2MT' 2-6-0 No 78026, Newton Stewart-Whithorn freight, 27 May 1964.**

Now out to Galloway in south-west Scotland, where I always like to be. More's the pity that the direct line from Dumfries and its associated branches have gone. Let's recall them just a little.

The station known as New Galloway was about five miles from the town, a favourite place of mine with one main street that always brings to mind townships in cowboy films. The loco, which has just completed its run through 14 miles of inhospitable open country (broken only by the lonely loops at Loch Skerrow and Gatehouse of Fleet), necessitated by selfish land-owning interests when the line was built - how many millions of passengers have been inconvenienced as a result - approaches the tablet apparatus. There is a large crane in the yard.

At the other end of this bleak section the station name of Creetown can be seen on the glass housing the oil lamp. The fireman is ready with the tablet. Milk used to be sent from here by rail; on my last visit a road tanker, bearing a Middlesex registration, was just setting out.

Wigtown used to give its name to the county hereabouts. Here's the station, and the children have turned out to witness the twice-weekly train. This must have been a tradition, for in a later picture, with infants, they race the goods on their tricycles. On that occasion boxes of cornflakes had been unloaded from a van.

Alan and I are on board during the shunting at Sorbie - with the wrong headcode I am advised - and the shunter is leaning on his pole. Milk traffic originated here too. *3211/3201/2949/3204*

**Ravenswood Junction, Borders; LNER 'B1' 4-6-0 No 61242, southbound freight, 18 July 1963.**
This junction on the Waverley route (see text on page 93) was for the South Berwickshire Railway which originally ran not just to Greenlaw but also to Duns and Reston. The floods of 1948 breached the formation and it was never repaired. *2915*

**Dalrymple Viaduct, Strathclyde; LMS '5MT' 2-6-0 No 42861, Ayr-Waterside Colliery coal empties, 27 August 1965.**
This train is on its way to Dalmellington - or is it going only as far as Waterside Colliery? When I rode it with Alan two years earlier it happened to be a Tuesday (26 May) and the guard advised us that only on Tuesdays did they make the through journey; on other days they played cards at the colliery. Imagine our surprise, therefore, to find at the terminus a fully signalled level crossing, with staff, and a Station Master wearing gold braid to greet the once-a-week service to his station! This is what Dr Beeching should have tackled. There was no shortage of staff at HQ in those days to carry out the changes needed. Trains still run to an open-cast site on the branch. *3505*

**Edinburgh, Princes Street Gardens, Lothian; LNER 'V2' 2-6-2 No 60931, 8.40 am Dundee (Tay Bridge)-Edinburgh (Waverley), and NBR 'J36' 0-6-0 No 65243, pw train.**
**Same location; LNER 'A3' 4-6-2 No 60090 *Grand Parade*, 11.23 am Edinburgh (Waverley)-Cowdenbeath, both 19 May 1957.**
The permanent way train is the common feature of these two pictures taken on a Sunday morning. The first shows ordinary open goods wagons with an LNER or BR brake and an LMS brake at the rear. The other is 'hybar' stock loaded with spent ballast, probably laboriously shovelled in by hand. These are followed by two three-plank dropside wagons. Later I made my first visit to the Forth Bridge. 959/960

64577

**Left** *Edzell, Tayside; NBR 'J37' 0-6-0 No 64577, freight to Brechin.*
***Below left*** **Careston, Tayside; BR '5MT' 4-6-0 No 73008, freight to Forfar, both 19 May 1964.**
Now we move north of the Firth of Forth to the area near Brechin. Just look at the wasteland which the loco is shunting at Careston. The train ran only on a Tuesday. There were no regular workings to Edzell by the time of this picture but the loading gauge still stood guard and the grass still grew! See page 93. *3167/3163*

***Right*** **Alford, Grampian; NBR 'J36' 0-6-0 No 65303, freight to Kittybrewster, 2 June 1959.**
***Below*** **Inveramsay, Grampian; same locomotive, Macduff-Kittybrewster freight, 1 June 1959.**
Another loading gauge marks the entry to the yard at Alford, and a Great North of Scotland Railway signal is controlled from a box of that company.

The previous day the same locomotive had brought us from Macduff to Inverurie (see page 94) and has just reached the junction with the Aberdeen/Inverness at Inveramsay. Here another GNofS signal controls the way ahead, though the Guard is busy at the ground frame so that the loco can do some shunting. Passenger stock stands on the right. *1687/1677*

65303

65303

**Left** Wartle, Grampian; NBR 'J36' 0-6-0 No 65303, 8.25 am Macduff-Kittybrewster freight. **Below left** Rothie Norman, Grampian; same locomotive, same train, both 1 June 1959.
Earlier in the trip we had called at these two stations. The Guard is waiting for me to advise him when photography is complete so that we can proceed! There are both upper and lower quadrant signals at both locations, and Rothie Norman has a Great North of Scotland signal box. *1676/1674*

**Right** Locheilside, Highland; NBR 'J36' 0-6-0 No 65300, Glenfinnan-Fort William freight. **Below** Near Glenfinnan, Highland, GNR 'K2' 2-6-0 No 61788 *Loch Rannoch*, Fort William-Mallaig freight, both 5 June 1959.
Where better to finish our review of freight traffic than on the West Highland Extension? The building at Locheilside is a station typical of the style on the road to Mallaig. The climb towards Glenfinnan is now lost in the trees; even then Alan and I had a hard scramble up the hillside to see the fish train headed by the named 'K2' with side-window cab. *1708/1706*

# 10. Holiday traffic

Until the motor car became part of the family furniture most holidays in the UK were taken by train, mainly to the seaside, out and back on a few Saturdays at the height of the summer. The railways were geared up to cope with this traffic, largely of their own creation, and to do so they maintained sufficient rolling-stock to meet the demand of a peak Summer Saturday. Almost any locomotives were brought into service to haul the coaches.

Needless to say, when the economists appeared at BR in the late '50s in anticipation of a Beeching, they saw an easy way of demonstrating their expertise by making savings in the number of coaches on the books. This policy, probably sound at first, has continued to such an extent that today there is little margin, if any, for breakdown or overcrowding.

These extra holiday trains often followed routes not taken by any other regular services and provided a bit of excitement on cross-country secondary lines; they even ran on tracks from which passenger services had been withdrawn. Some involved operating practices unfamiliar at intermediate stations. I recall being on a train from the East Coast which divided at Melton Mowbray into portions for Leicester and Nottingham. This occurred only on a handful of Saturdays and I heard a sigh of relief from behind my carriage as it finished for the year.

Trains from the North East to Blackpool would climb over Stainmore (page 142) and use the West Coast Main Line from Tebay to Preston. Here mothers would tell their children that the journey was nearly over when, about 20 minutes later, they would come through the station again having completed a circuit via Todd Lane Junction to avoid reversal.

Shirebrook South had lost its regular passenger service in 1931 but I saw a train from Skegness terminate there on 11 August 1962. The buildings had been reduced to rubble but a Ticket Collector appeared on his bicycle, unlocked a gate on to the platform and steadfastly looked at everyone's ticket, thus creating a long queue of people impatient to get home.

The two lines I particularly associate with holiday trains are the former Lancashire, Derbyshire & East Coast, which survives in part as a route from Shirebrook to the High Marnham Power Station, and the former Great Northern/London & North Western Joint Line with its branch from Marefield Junction to the terminus at Leicester (Belgrave Road), which has been abandoned.

Harry, Alan and myself travelled from King's Cross to Bradford (Exchange) on 5 September 1964. We changed first at Grantham and then, after a ride through Leadenham to Lincoln, we took the holiday train via Edwinstowe (page 131) to Penistone. It was very crowded. From there we completed our journey on another holiday train, from Bournemouth. This was to prove a god-send at Denby Dale to crowds wishing suddenly to leave the Pie Festival on account of a freak summer storm. Normally the train would be express to Huddersfield, but extra stops were hastily arranged. It was virtually empty by this stage and provided far more accommodation than the two-car DMU normally employed on this line. On arrival at Denby Dale station we could see the queue of would-be passengers stretching down to the road below the viaduct, and only a few could be allowed on the platform at any one time because of the condition of the coping stones, so our progress became very slow.

My journey by train to Leicester (Belgrave Road), with Harry, began at King's Cross on 5 September 1959. We changed at Retford, where the fly-under had yet to be provided for east-west trains, so congestion was rife, and took a holiday service, via the Clarborough Junction-Sykes Junction direct route, going wrong line over the Trent bridge at Torksey, to Lincoln. We then followed in a DMU to Firsby and another to Boston where the Leicester train appeared. We had to stand in the corridor as far as Melton Mowbray North. At Thurnby & Scraptoft station (closed to passengers in 1957) we drew to a stand while the Guard hastened to a public phone box nearby. I later learned that he had rung Belgrave Road to ascertain if it was safe for us to proceed, ie had the train from Skegness (as opposed to Mablethorpe) settled into its platform, as the signalling was suspect!

The sets of coaches for these two trains, the only ones regularly to use the terminus, and then only on Summer Saturdays (and, one set only, on Summer Sundays), apparently remained there throughout the year. A locomotive would be attached on a Friday to warm one set before lunch, and the other in the afternoon. Geoff Hunt and I used to stay in Melton Mowbray over some weekends especially to see these trains on the Joint Line. At breakfast time we would see two 'B1' locomotives, tender first, hauling a brake-van with the two guards *en route* from Colwick to Belgrave Road. At dinner we would see them returning. Meanwhile we would photograph the Mablethorpe and Skegness outward and return trains (see pages 129 and 130). The condition of the track at Lowesby was such that the engine would lean from side to side; goodness knows what it was like in Thurnby Tunnel (page 154)! The trains were withdrawn from 9 September 1962.

**Near Commins Coch, Powys; GWR '90XX' 4-4-0 No 9018 and unidentified GWR 'Manor' 4-6-0, 11.00 am Aberystwyth-Manchester (London Road), 22 August 1959.**

The height of the August weekend holiday traffic on the Cambrian, and everything is pressed into service. I had hoped to see a 'Dukedog' in an open landscape so that its fascinating appearance could be fully captured, but we did not know which train would be so hauled and inevitably it was the one where the surroundings constrained the view. Never mind, it's nice anyway with its LMS stock. As pilot engine it would have been detached at Talerddig summit (see overleaf) and returned to Machynlleth. *1801*

Near Commins Coch, Powys; GWR 'Manor' 4-6-0 No 7829 *Ramsbury Manor* and BR '4MT' 4-6-0 No 75026, 12.30 pm Aberystwyth-Birmingham (Snow Hill).
Talerddig, Powys; 10.45 am Manchester (London Road)-Aberystwyth banked by BR '2MT' 2-6-0 No 78006, and GWR '2251' 0-6-0 No 2233, pilot off 12.40 pm Aberystwyth-Crewe, both 22 August 1959.

In the upper picture you can see the bridge from which the photo on the previous page was taken, looking away from the camera. It was here that I had hoped to see the 'Dukedog', but perhaps the double-heading makes up for it.

At Talerddig summit another pilot engine is waiting to return westwards. Meanwhile, and less commonly, a train of mixed stock has been banked from Moat Lane Junction. *1806/1804*

**Near Troutbeck, Cumbria; LMS '2MT' 2-6-0 No 46488, Keswick-Manchester (Exchange), 15 August 1964.**
Still in the west but much farther north, the line from Penrith to Workington saw far fewer extra holiday trains, so they were of that much greater interest when they came. When I returned two years later this train, and other loco-hauled services, used the other track in both directions due to a weak bridge. *3298*

**Scarborough, North Yorks; LNER 'B1' 4-6-0 No 61084, 10.10 am to London (King's Cross), 23 May 1960.**
There were so many trains to Scarborough at the height of the summer holiday season that most of the intermediate stations were closed in 1930 so as to dispense with the slower stopping services which got in the way of the through traffic - or so the story goes. Certainly I have never envied the signalman at Malton who, prior to the building of the bypass in recent years, had to make a judgement between the competing claims of road and rail traffic to and from the coast at his level crossing. As he was paid to pass the trains, the cars would have to wait, but there must have been a delicate balancing act between the two streams in the early 1960s. In addition, there are two road junctions adjacent to the crossing, as well as the old A64. The awnings above the platform at Scarborough have been removed, but there remains the longest station seat in the kingdom. *1949*

ALTON TOWERS

GENTLEMEN
GAMLINGAY
1X63
45379

**_Left_ Alton Towers, Staffs; LMS '4MT' 2-6-4T No 42378, Macclesfield-Uttoxeter, 6 May 1961.**
Alton Towers is now more famous for its fun fair - at the top of the hill to the right of the picture - and the station (closed in 1965) is available for letting from the Landmark Trust. The setting is delectable with a fairylike castle on the skyline behind the camera. It's also an ideal hideaway for parking the surplus stock. The trains here used to connect Uttoxeter with Macclesfield by way of the Churnet Valley and a very pleasant ride it was too. There is a preservation movement at Cheddleton today and the track survives between Leek Brook and Kingsley, but only on a care-and-maintenance basis. *2397*

**_Below left_ Gamlingay, Cambs; LMS Class '5' 4-6-0 No 45379, diverted Yarmouth (Vauxhall)-Birmingham (New Street), 8 June 1963.**
Just look at the paraphernalia on the down platform by the BR blue enamel nameboard (ER) mounted in an LMS frame. The station is uncharacteristic of the LNWR - those between Potton and Old North Road all had shelters on the up side, and this is quite unique for the company. It is oil-lit, and the platform is composed partly of small bricks. *2902*

**_Right_ Radcliffe-on-Trent, Notts; LNER 'B1' 4-6-0 No 61188, Nottingham (Victoria)-Skegness, 31 August 1963.**
**_Below_ Melton Mowbray North, Leics; LNER 'B1' 4-6-0 No 61141, Leicester (Belgrave Road)-Skegness, 18 July 1959.**
Although the posters at Radcliffe-on-Trent commend holidays in Scarborough and Broadstairs, all the passengers in these two pictures are probably making for Skegness, which was brought to life by the railway in the summer. Gas lighting, I think, and a neat building complete with fire buckets.

Once a magnificent building at Melton Mowbray, it has clearly seen better days when the awnings were fully glazed. There was a wide stone staircase, as in a baronial hall, to each platform, and these had 1st and 2nd Class waiting rooms and, if I recall correctly, one each for both ladies and gentlemen. I had visited the station the previous evening; the place was wide open to public access but unlit, and in the dark it was very weird; a goods train stood there while its loco sizzled and took water from the column on the northbound platform. *2980/1738*

**Lowesby, Leics; LNER 'B1' 4-6-0 No 61390, Mablethorpe-Leicester (Belgrave Road).**
**Near Marefield Junction, Leics; LNER 'B1' 4-6-0 No 61088, Skegness-Leicester (Belgrave Road), both 27 August 1960.**

I used to love to visit the branch to Leicester (Belgrave Road) (see the text on page 124), and in particular Lowesby station (closed 1957). This was over the hill from the village, at the end of a long approach road in a remote setting with some railway cottages. Sadly it had been visited by vandals on motor cycles even then (1959) who, being brought before the magistrates, were fined only 10s 6d each. Evidently the buildings were valued at about £3! No wonder we have the problems we do today. Be that as it may, the atmosphere there fascinated me, and to watch the summer trains come along the grass-grown and uneven track never ceased to amuse.

Do notice in the lower picture how the weed-killing train has clearly turned back on both tracks (was it propelled there?) just in front of the returning train at Marefield. I am willing to bet that somewhere in the engineer's records it stipulated this, because beyond that point (where the trees mark the former west-to-south curve) the track became exclusively Great Northern property rather than that of the GNR and LNWR Committee. This must have happened 40 years after both had ceased to exist. *2215/2218*

**Edwinstowe, Notts; LNER 'K3' 2-6-0 No 61826, 2.11 pm Skegness-Basford (North), 11 August 1962.**
**Tuxford (Central), Notts; LNER 'K3' 2-6-0 No 61957, Leicester (Central)-Scarborough via Bridlington, 11 August 1962.**
Not quite as fascinating as the line on the opposite page but nevertheless of interest was the Lancashire, Derbyshire & East Coast route. Whereas the trains passed non-stop through Lowesby, here they called at Edwinstowe until 1964, despite its closure to other traffic more than nine years before. The picture shows a complete tidy station for the two or three trains that called each Saturday during the summer peak. I suspect that relations between the NUM and NUR has something to do with this situation.

The train at Tuxford Central is about to take a spur northwards to join the East Coast Main Line. I have a picture of that, but only with a main line-train. The LD&ECR now runs just to High Marnham Power Station. *2725/2730*

# 11. Landscapes

For me it is the train in the landscape that makes the perfect picture. Writing about my collection recently, someone expressed his 'disappointment to find that there are no "solo loco on shed" portraits', and he is almost right. The loco is a means to an end as far as I am concerned, not an end in itself. The photograph at Login (page 135) is an excellent example. We had stood on the platform looking up at the field from which the picture was subsequently taken, and were guided to it by the helpful porter. Meanwhile, the first illustration (opposite) provides continuity with the last feature as it shows a holiday train from Swansea to Pokesdown.

Most of my photographs are indexed in geographical order along the respective routes, starting at North Pole Junction near Olympia, London, going around the former Southern Region and then heading west, then east and finally north to end at Oban after taking account of Wick and Thurso.

In securing these pictures I have studied the 1-inch OS maps and their modern counterparts in great detail, and have tried not to visit the same place twice, though this is often unavoidable. If I have been to a certain bridge over the line, then next time I will go to the next bridge and so on.

If I can find an elevated view with a panoramic background then I'm really happy. I do not carry secateurs or saws with me, but a pair of stout gloves is handy to remove obtrusive thistles.

The picture of Pitcombe church (page 136) tells a story. My other principle hobby is recorded music, and my late father before me used to entertain friends as I do now. One of these moved to Bruton in Somerset, and we lost contact. When Ian Cantlon and I arrived at Pitcombe we could hear the sound of the organ in the church. As we descended the hill after taking the photo a lady appeared from the church door with some sheet music. I somehow knew it was our old friend but I could only stare at her and remain dumb. A lost opportunity to renew friendship.

The photograph near Market Weighton (page 134) gives the impression of tranquillity, as it should. But I felt anything but tranquil that day. I had just bought a new car, and drove there the day after its 1,000-mile service. When I started it that morning I discovered a large pool of oil under the vehicle. A nearby garage topped it up and tightened some nut or other which had evidently not been fixed properly. I was advised to keep an eye on the oil level and near Market Weighton I found that I was running short again. Another visit to a garage (bearing in mind that the train was getting closer), another top-up and another tightening of nuts and this time we were all right. It was essential to feel secure, as later that evening I drove from Whitby to Southam in Warwickshire in readiness for the next day's special!

Chedworth (page 134) brings back memories of the *On Railways* programme as my first broadcast, live, was about the run-down of the Midland & South Western Junction Railway. Unbeknown to me a senior BBC executive lived there and exercised his dog by walking through the tunnel. I took a portable tape recorder with me and began at the southern end of the line, entering the now defunct post office at East Grafton to seek opinions from the customers about the service. Although Grafton & Burbage station was still open they denied this and implied that I was too late. In Withington at the other end of the line I casually spoke to a stranger in the street only to be told that he was the son of the then Speaker of the House of Commons. An object lesson, perhaps. I joined the train from Cirencester (Watermoor) to Andoversford and obtained views from some of the passengers. In the event - on 22 July 1959 - only my own contribution was broadcast.

My first journey to Killin (page 137), with Alan, was on 24 May 1957 in a train so crowded that I was wedged in a compartment of its one coach. It was a Friday evening and people were coming out of Glasgow and Edinburgh for the weekend. The previous evening, in Pitlochry, we had been made to look small by the receptionist of the hotel because we were travelling by rail (the door giving direct access to the station had been locked) and thus could not give a car registration number. I was therefore feeling apprehensive about our arrival in Killin. I need not have worried. The door at Pitlochry is now back in use!

**Downton Tunnel, Wilts; unidentified BR '4MT' 2-6-0, Swansea (High Street)-Pokesdown, 2 July 1960.**
The day was spent in the car photographing summer Saturday extras in the south of England. And what more typical than this one, using the sleepy branch line from Alderbury Junction (near Salisbury) to West Moors (near Wimborne), and entering the cutting that leads to the north portal of Downton Tunnel? *2085*

**Chedworth, Glos; unidentified SR 'U' 2-6-0, 1.52 pm Cheltenham (St James's)-Southampton (Terminus), 24 September 1960.**
**Near Market Weighton, Humberside; LNER 'K4' 2-6-0 No 3442 *The Great Marquess* and LNER 'K1' 2-6-0 No 62005, RCTS special Leeds-Whitby, 6 March 1965.**

Two really rural scenes, one in a village where the train is hiding among the houses. The other is in open downland where the sheep are feeding on the last of the turnips. *2248/3370*

**Login, Dyfed; GWR '45XX' 2-6-2T No 4557, 4.00 pm Whitland-Cardigan, 31 May 1962.**
As I record in the text, the porter at Login station helped us to find this super spot from which to photograph the train. The scenery is typical of the whole line to Cardigan. 2678

*Left* Glastonbury, Somerset; LMS '2MT' 2-6-2T No 41272, 4.48 pm Evercreech Junction-Highbridge, 29 March 1962.
*Below left* Pitcombe, Somerset; LMS '8F' 2-8-0 No 48309, LCGB 'Wessex Downsman' (Waterloo-Bristol-Bournemouth), 4 April 1965.
The Somerset & Dorset line, too, ran through superb scenery all the way - in the upper picture the tor on the hill in the right background identifies the approach to Glastonbury. I refer to the picture at Pitcombe in the text (page 132). *2602/3390*

*Right* Cwm Prysor, Gwynedd; GWR '58XX' 0-4-2T No 5810, 9.15 am Blaenau Ffestiniog-Bala, 13 May 1958.
*Below* Near Killin, Central Region; CR '2P' 0-4-4T No 55268, 11.05 am Killin-Killin Junction, 14 July 1961.
Two mountainous scenes to conclude - one in Wales and the other in Scotland. The 9.15 am from Blaenau Ffestiniog to Bala ran on Tuesdays, Thursdays and Saturdays only; it is just passing a trolley used by the local lengthman and platelayer in this lovely environment. The lower ground to the left of the locomotive is now under Llyn Celyn.

The little train from Killin ran just to the junction with the Callandar & Oban; the Caledonian there was so mean that when the station opened and replaced its own stopping place at the summit of Glen Ogle they supplied a new nameboard only for the word 'Junction', the word 'Killin' having to be transferred and mated up! *1284/2451*

# 12. Viaducts and bridges

*Above* **Loch nan Uamh Viaduct, Highland; LNER 'K1/1' 2-6-0 No 61997 *MacCailin Mor*, 4.50 pm Fort William-Mallaig, 4 June 1959.**
*Right* **Banavie Swing Bridge, Highland; LNER 'K1' 2-6-0 No 62012,same train, 29 May 1957.**
The times of trains rarely changed until recent years. Hence although these pictures were taken two years apart, the train is still the 4.50 pm from Fort William to Mallaig. Since the introduction of radio signalling, the West Highland and its Extension have been controlled throughout from the signal box by the swing bridge. The photograph there appeared on the cover of The Railway Magazine in July 1958; according to Brian Stephenson, who should know about these matters, it is sharper than the equivalent taken by the distinguished photographer W. J. V. Anderson! *1700/1021*

*Left* **Killiecrankie Viaduct, Tayside; LMS Class '5' 4-6-0 No 45068, 4.00 pm Perth-Inverness, 23 May 1957.**
This viaduct, between Pitlochry and Blair Atholl, is 169 yards long, and to reach this spot Alan and I took the bus back up the valley from Pitlochry. Fortunately its timetable fitted in with the trains we wished to photograph. Today the scene is lost in the trees. *991*

**Tay Bridge, Tayside; LNER 'B1' 4-6-0 No 61103, 12.46 pm Dundee (Tay Bridge)-Edinburgh (Waverley) via Tayport, 20 May 1957.**
**Royal Border Bridge, Berwick-upon-Tweed, Northumberland; BR '2MT' 2-6-0 No 78049, 9.30 am from Kelso, 20 July 1963.**

How fortunate that I photographed the Tay Bridge in the days of steam, from the platform of the Esplanade station (which closed in 1939). The bridge is 2 miles 364 yards long. The Royal Border Bridge at Berwick-upon-Tweed is a mere 720 yards, but the train from St Boswells still looks quite lost. *965/2933*

**Shankend Viaduct, Borders; unidentified LNER 'B1' 4-6-0 and LMS 'Royal Scot' 4-6-0, Bathgate-Cowley carflats, 20 July 1963.**
**Great Water of Fleet Viaduct, Dumfries & Galloway; unidentified BR '4MT' 2-6-0, 3.40 pm Stranraer (Town)-Dumfries, 26 May 1964.**
Viaducts in the east and west of Scotland. Shankend is on the Waverley route from Carlisle to Edinburgh (closed in 1969). I had gone there to see the through express from London (St Pancras) and had the bonus of this south-bound company train. Later I saw the local set down railway wives, returning from shopping in Hawick, by the cottages at Whitrope Summit (they had a scheduled stop in the Working Timetable).

By the time that this train passed over Great Water of Fleet Viaduct, I had abandoned tape recording (see the photograph on page 4) and concentrated on taking in the bleak scenery. The station at Gatehouse of Fleet was nearly two miles west of here and some six miles from the place it purported to serve. The Guard of the goods had 25 minutes in the Working Timetable to deliver milk to the community, which was at the end of the B796, a distinction it shared with Bordon station in Hampshire, at the end of B3002. What a useless piece of information! *2939/3197*

***Above*** **Belah Viaduct; LMS '2MT' 2-6-0 No 46422 banked by LMS '4MT' 2-6-0 No 43018, eastbound freight, 28 May 1960.**
***Left*** **Stainmore, Co Durham; summit signboard, 12 August 1961.**
It is soon after one o'clock. A black cloud has appeared above the hills to the right and moves from left to right before coming towards us. Alan sighs with relief, for he had little faith in freight train timings and had expected to be here far longer. In fact the train ran at the time given to us by the signalman at Lartington Viaduct, where we had seen a DMU earlier, and his experience was better than any book. This fantastic structure over the River Belah was 347 yards long. Built by Gilkes, Wilson & Co, it is now no more. *2001/2509*

***Above right*** **Crumlin Viaduct, Gwent; GWR '56XX' 0-6-2T No 6661, 11.15 am Aberdare-Pontypool Road, 23 March 1961.**
***Right*** **River Wye, Whitney-on-Wye, Hereford & Worcs; GWR '57XX' 0-6-0PT No 3768, 6.00 pm Brecon-Hereford, 28 May 1962.**
During the course of 550 yards Crumlin Viaduct, now also dismantled, took the trains from Neath to Pontypool Road above those which still link Cardiff and Rhymney and over the Ebbw River.

Beneath the Brecon-Hereford train is the shadow of the toll bridge on the old road to Hay-on-Wye that everyone can now easily bypass. A storm is brewing and the sky is quite threatening. *2338/2659*

**Connel Ferry Bridge, Strathclyde; CR '2P' 0-4-4T No 55263, 10.45 am Ballachulish-Oban, 18 July 1961.**
This 460-yard-long bridge is at the mouth of Loch Etive and used to be shared by road and rail, the signalman crossing the bridge on his cycle to lock the gate against motorists and the like when the train was due. I remember being present when a lorry driver found that his vehicle was too wide to cross and had to return to Tyndrum and go round via Glencoe. Despite his language I helped him to reverse and turn round. It never ceases to surprise me how few lorry drivers know their vehicle's height or weight on any particular journey. When they stop to seek directions from you, ask these questions first lest there is a weak or low bridge ahead, and find out for yourself! *2465*

**River Hamble, Bursledon, Hants; BR '3MT' 2-6-2T No 82015, 11.18 am Portsmouth & Southsea-Andover Junction, 7 September 1957.**
The bridge over the Hamble has little artistic merit in my eyes, but it is often surrounded by a myriad of boats from nearby marinas, a status symbol of success in the South East. *1079*

**Knucklas Viaduct, Powys; LMS '4MT' 2-6-4T No 42390, 10.25 am Swansea (Victoria)-Shrewsbury, 19 August 1959.**
This viaduct, 214 yards long, has castellated ends and crosses tributaries of the River Teme, famed by its inclusion in Houseman's poems and Vaughan-Williams's music which mirror this lovely countryside. I feel that the viaduct adds to and provides a focal point for the local environment. *2715*

**Britannia Tubular Bridge, Gwynedd; LMS Class '5' 4-6-0 No 45144, eastbound freight, 24 May 1962.**
I sense that Mike Esau's artistic temperament is mildly offended by the sight of a lion riding on a wagon! Whatever, this fine bridge of Robert Stephenson, 460 yards long, has been transformed following an accidental fire, and now carries road traffic above the trains. *2639*

**Harringworth Viaduct, Leics; unidentified BR '5MT' 4-6-0, London (St Pancras)-Sheffield express, 18 July 1959.**

**Yarm Viaduct, Cleveland; unidentified WD '8F' 2-8-0, northbound light engine, 12 April 1965.**

Two really long viaducts, over the Welland (between Corby and Oakham) and the Tees (between Northallerton and Eaglescliff). Harringworth is 1,275 yards long in brick, and repairs have not always been carried out in sympathy with the original colour so that the valley has been given a motley appearance, presumably through lack of interest by the civil engineer who has probably assumed for years that the freight-only line above would close and it could be demolished. Better were it to be put on the local tourist trail.

Yarm, 1,034 yards long (and 55 feet high), is hidden behind the High Street - more's the pity! *1750/3398*

**Moorswater Viaduct, Cornwall; unidentified GWR 'Grange' 4-6-0, 4.20 pm Penzance-Plymouth, 8 July 1960.**
**Pensford Viaduct, Avon; GWR '57XX' 0-6-0PT No 9668, 2.53 pm Bristol (Temple Meads)-Frome, 16 May 1959.**
This section is brought to an end by two viaducts in the West Country. Moorswater, 268 yards long and crossing the Looe River, carries trains between Penzance and Plymouth, which probably go to more varied destinations than on any other line in the country. Passengers were once allowed to travel on the mineral line below if they paid for their umbrellas.

Finally, the fine structure at Pensford (330 yards long) on the North Somerset Line from Bristol to Radstock and Frome. Norman Simmonds showed me his picture of this at the REC Clubrooms one day and I wasn't satisfied until I had captured it myself. And here it is! *2098/1612*

# 13. Waterside

By the time that I came to take the picture (below) of the train near Cray, the service over the Neath & Brecon had been reduced to one return working each weekday, augmented by a further one on Saturdays. You see the 4.10 pm ex-Neath, and as soon as it had passed Bob and Phyl Kirkland and myself it stopped and the driver called out to see that we had managed to take the photo we wanted. I'm sure that he would have set the train back had we wished. The Guard was leaning out of the window of a 1st Class compartment smoking a cigarette. Needless to say, there was no one else on board. With so little custom, the yard at Riverside station had become grass-grown and had acquired the unkempt air so familiar in the post-Beeching period. On a visit from City & Guilds to the Headquarters of a major company, Bob had great satisfaction in finding a chauffeur-driven limousine to meet him off the train in these decaying surroundings!

Until I visited Neyland (page 150) I had assumed that the expresses steaming out of Paddington with roofboards naming places in West Wales were heading for important centres. Some, no doubt, were, but I beg to question the inclusion of this terminus, which closed in 1964. Alan and I were the only passengers on this train which, because of its London destination, was so long that the Guard had to go out into the station forecourt to give the 'Right away' to the driver, who otherwise could not see him on the curved platform. There were no other staff about.

Kingswear is now the terminus of the Paignton & Dartmouth Railway. My picture (page 149) was taken on a Sunday in BR days and I had parked my Morris Minor with other cars whose occupants were admiring the view. Hugh Davies and I then crossed to Dartmouth by ferry and took lunch (incidentally, in my case a meal of bad pork that resulted in the worst night I have had yet in my life). Returning later we noticed a constable standing by the car, which was now in splendid isolation. Did we acknowledge it to be ours? Yes. The policeman was so nice. Had we realised, he asked, that we had parked in a turning circle for lorries? No. Well, if you come again please park it elsewhere! I've not been back yet.

Of all the trains I miss since closure I have little doubt that the 9.55 am Moat Lane Junction to Brecon (seen at Llanfaredd on page 151) is top of the list. Admittedly, every time I used it was a sunny day, but the joy of travelling through the mountains and returning time and again to the sparkling waters of the River Wye is unforgettable. I stood once, with Geoff Hunt, on a rock midstream to photograph a train crossing near Llyswen and the freshness of the water lingers with me still. We used to change at Talyllyn Junction and go over Torpantau to South Wales. Arrival at Newport was always such an anti-climax.

The photo on page 153 of the 'A4' in the rock cutting south of Aberdeen is an exception to an unwritten rule, ie that the sun goes in as the train comes by. In this case, with Ian, it had rained all morning, but a freak ray of sunlight emerged from the clouds as the express appeared and lit it up. It then rained again for the rest of the day.

**Near Cray, Powys; GWR '57XX' 0-6-0PT No 9786, 4.10 pm Neath-Brecon, 23 March 1961.** The water here is in the Cray Reservoir, and the situation is described in the text above. *2341*

**Kingswear, Devon; GWR 'King' 4-6-0 No 6025 *King Henry III*, 1.08 pm to London (Paddington), 10 July 1960.**
The Dart estuary is featured in this picture, which is so vintage as to show paddle steamers berthed. There is a wealth of detail here illustrating a GWR terminus, and the edge of the turntable is visible on the lower right. I'm told that the signal box has gone and that there is road access to a marina through lifting barriers but, of course, preservationists have restored the train service. *2108*

*Left* **Neyland, Dyfed; GWR 'County' 4-6-0 No 1020 *County of Monmouth*, 2.30 pm to London (Paddington), 19 May 1961.**
Had the Hobbs Point ferry not run late, Alan and I would have been on the DMU which we watched depart, from the deck of the ship. In the event I'm glad, for this interesting view resulted and is mentioned in the text (page 148). Neyland, at the mouth of the Cleddau, was an early terminal for the Irish crossing prior to the opening of Fishguard. *2417*

*Below* **St Briavels, Gwent; GWR '54XX' 0-6-0PT No 6412, southbound freight, 2 June 1962.**
*Opposite page* **Near Llanfaredd, Powys; LMS '2MT' 2-6-0 No 46516, 9.55 am Moat Lane Junction-Brecon, 28 May 1962.**
The River Wye is the link here. The next call for the Saturday morning goods is Tintern on its way from Monmouth to Chepstow.

The full-page illustration opposite is much farther north, near Builth Wells, and features my favourite train - the 9.55 am Moat Lane Junction to Brecon. *2688/2663*

**Severn Bridge, Glos; unidentified GWR '43XX' 2-6-0, 9.10 am Cardiff (General)-Portsmouth Harbour, 22 February 1959.**
**Severn Bridge, Glos; GWR '54XX' 0-6-0PT No 5417, 1.55 pm Berkeley Road-Lydney Town, 6 May 1958.**
During a thick fog on the night of 25 October 1960 a tanker loaded with oil collided with one of the piers of this bridge. One pier and the two spans supported by it collapsed and it was never restored. To pass high above the waters of the Severn on a sunny day, with extensive views in all directions, was an experience I am glad I never missed and I'm sorry that it is denied to subsequent generations. The bridge, which carried only a single track, was nearly three-quarters of a mile long and was brought into use in 1879. It had 22 bowstring girder spans (one of which could be opened for the passage of ships on the Gloucester & Sharpness Canal) and 14 masonry approach arches. The train in the upper picture is a Sunday diversion due to engineering work in the Severn Tunnel; the lower view is of the basic service from Berkeley Road (between Bristol and Gloucester) to Lydney. *1520/1243*

**Aberdeen Docks, Grampian; GNSR 'Z5' 0-4-2T No 68192, shunting timber wagons, 22 May 1957.**
**Near Aberdeen, Grampian; LNER 'A4' 4-6-2 No 60024 *Kingfisher*, 1.30 pm Aberdeen-Glasgow (Buchanan Street), 31 August 1965.**
The North Sea provides the water in the docks at Aberdeen and by the lighthouse. And they are really contrasting trains: the wagons being propelled into Waterloo goods, and the passenger express. Note in the upper picture that there are no skirts on the loco for street running; note also the cobbled street and the range of vintage advertisements on the right. *3514/984*

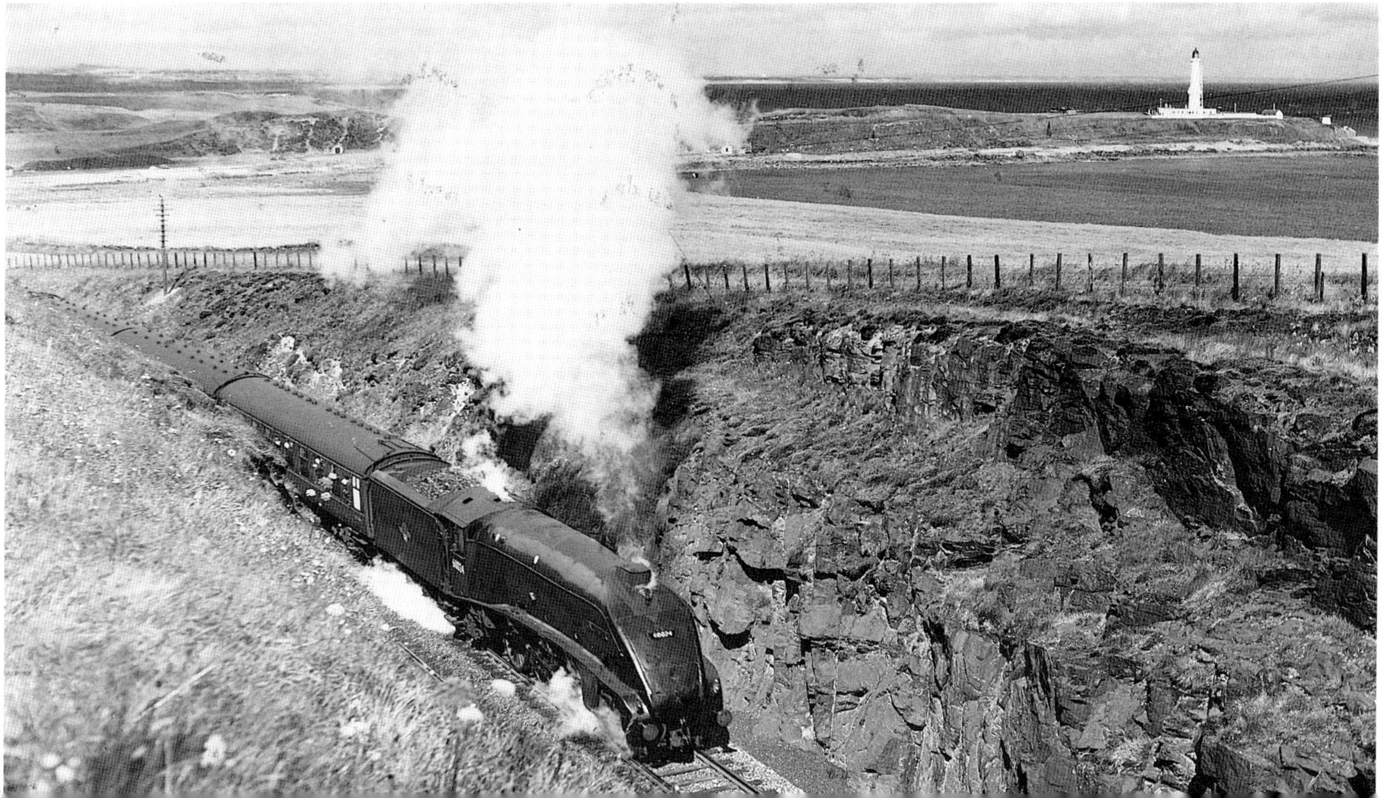

# 14. Tunnels and level crossings

While Ludlow station remains open and, with almost an hourly regular interval service northbound alternately to Liverpool and Manchester and southbound to Cardiff, has a better service probably than ever before, the little push-and-pull train in my earlier picture (page 74) is the like of which we shall never see again. It is 3rd Class only and working the 3.15 pm from Leominster to Craven Arms. The duty involves returning at 4.05 as far as Woofferton, then making a sortie down the branch to Tenbury Wells. It reappears on the main line at 5.52 and goes back to Leominster. Earlier in the day it had performed this itinerary in reverse.

Earlier we saw a holiday train approaching Downton Tunnel (page 133); now we see the southern portal (page 156) and the stopping service from Salisbury to Bournemouth West. The narrow chalk cutting was very liable to slipping.

I referred earlier (page 124) to the possible condition of the track in Thurnby Tunnel. The Sunday morning excursion to Skegness (below) has passed through safely; this is almost my only picture taken standing on the track, which I deplore, and, prior to hearing the approach of the train, I kept walking back round the blind corner behind me to assure myself that I was not about to be mown down and give a driver nightmares.

The quieter the line the more dangerous it tends to be. When issuing a track permit for the Upton-on-Severn branch, the LMR stressed that they were testing new DMUs there and these could approach swiftly and silently. I was almost caught out at Ravenstone Wood Junction - a more isolated place than this, on the former Bedford to Northampton branch, would be hard to find - one Sunday morning when normally there was no traffic all day; but suddenly, up wind from round the corner came a light engine really hurtling along. Another occasion was near Yeovil Junction. I was walking beside the up line from Weymouth, then double track, and passing beneath a road bridge with a continuous retaining wall to a bridge under the West of England main line where there was limited clearance. Suddenly I picked up a sound and turned to find a Pannier tank and pick-up goods bearing down on me fast. I just managed to run out of the end right into a group of platelayers having a sandwich lunch. They remonstrated with me and I pacified them only by producing my track permit. A lesson was learned - never walk, even a short distance, in the direction of the traffic.

The signals illustrated at Nantgaredig and Rylstone (pages 156 and 157) bear witness to the companies that built the lines, the London & North Western and Midland respectively. The first was closed in 1963, and used to carry a fish train from Tenby to the Midlands mid-afternoon. The other remains for aggregate traffic from the nearby Swinden Quarry of Tarmac, which is carried regularly to a site at Hull. These are very heavy trains and substitute for a multitude of lorries.

***Left*** **Thurnby, Leics; LNER 'B1' 4-6-0 No 61141, Leicester (Belgrave Road)-Skegness, 19 July 1959.**

***Opposite page*** **Devizes Tunnel, Wilts; GWR '54XX' 0-6-0PT No 5416, 11.02 am Devizes-Patney & Chirton, 16 May 1959.**

I love the Devizes picture, with the little train on its short working to the junction at Patney & Chirton on the West of England main line. The junction station has been demolished but its footbridge survives to carry a path from one meadow to another. Devizes Tunnel was 190 yards long and, as you can see, it passed beneath the castle grounds, so the track could enter the station area immediately on the other side. There is even a little summerhouse with a straw roof. I'm on my way to the S&D and North Somerset lines.

The old signpost tells you the length of Thurnby Tunnel (see the text above). *1607/1751*

5416

**Downton Tunnel, Wilts; BR '4MT' 2-6-0 No 76038, 5.20 pm Salisbury-Bournemouth (West), 25 June 1955.**

Earlier (page 133) we saw the Saturday through train from Swansea approaching Downton Tunnel. Now we are at the southern portal with a local service. I'm on my way to Yelverton (for Princetown) (page 79) and this picture is on the same roll of film. It's one of the oldest in this book. *576*

**Nantgaredig, Dyfed; GWR '57XX' 0-6-0PT No 3693, 10.15 am Carmarthen-Llandeilo, 1 June 1962.**

Despite the ex-GWR locomotive, the signal at Nantgaredig clearly betrays the station's LNWR origins. *2679*

**Rylstone, North Yorks; LMS '4F' 0-6-0 No 44468, Grassington-Skipton freight, 25 May 1960.**
The little station at Rylstone is a gem and there is a Midland Railway ground frame as well as that company's signal. The goods has stopped whilst the guard opens the gates. *1972*

# 15. Signals and signal boxes

After my interlude with the platelayers near Yeovil Junction, I used my permit to walk northwards past the wartime junction (page 162), then between the Southern and Great Western lines, now used mainly for diversionary purposes between Castle Cary and Exeter St David's, until I came to Pen Mill station and ultimately Yeovil Town station (both page 161). I really enjoyed that day, partly because my visit was spontaneous. The morning had dawned sunny at Kingston-upon-Thames where I lived, so I rang my boss and asked if I could take the day off. He agreed and I was soon on board the 9 am from Waterloo to the West Country, which called at Surbiton in those days. I hadn't realised until that morning that the up and down 'Atlantic Coast Express' passed near Yeovil. I made my way home by the 'Pork Chop Train', which also called at Surbiton, at 9.49 pm.

I find the picture at Frocester (page 159) of interest in demonstrating how much quicker the trains run today compared with the one illustrated. It is about coffee-time on Sunday morning, yet the service is the 2.50 am from Leeds City to Bristol (Temple Meads).

I have already made reference to Three Cocks Junction, Heriot, Kirkby-in-Furness and Maiden Newton, which are illustrated in this section.

***Below*** **Broome, Shropshire; BR '4MT' 2-6-4T No 80097, 6.15 am Swansea (Victoria)-Shrewsbury, 28 July 1962.**
Somehow this picture epitomises what I have in mind for this section. Here we see a signal box of the London & North Western Railway, switched out, and one of that company's signals guarding the line ahead to Hopton Heath. It is amazing to me that these artefacts survived in regular use for a minimum of 40 years. For those with a trained eye they provide an interesting variation in the railway scene. *2714*

***Right*** **Kirkby-in-Furness, Cumbria; LMS '4MT' 2-6-4T No 42401, 8.30 am Carnforth-Workington, 1 June 1960.**
The LNWR is also represented at Kirkby by the elderly milk van behind the engine. Would it be the signalman's cycle at the foot of the steps of the Furness box? That company's seats are in evidence too. *2024*

***Below right*** **Frocester, Glos; BR '5MT' 4-6-0 No 73144, 2.50 am Leeds-Bristol (Temple Meads), 22 February 1959.**
The box at Frocester is typical Midland Railway, period 2, with an LMS name-board. Platform lighting is by oil-lamps. *1521*

KIRKBY
42401

FROCESTER
73144

**Holmsley, Hants; LSWR 'M7' 0-4-4T No 30111, 11.04 am Brockenhurst-Bournemouth (Central), 4 January 1958.**
**Verwood, Dorset; LSWR 'T9' 4-4-0 No 30288, 9.25 am Salisbury-Bournemouth (West), 1 October 1955.**
Two views back on the Southern. Holmsley is the alternative version of the LSWR small box with a large ventilator and ornate barge boards. At Verwood a free-standing poster illustrates suitcases and a spaniel, reminding you that you can take 'man's best friend' with you on holiday. The signal box is another version of the LSWR small box with hipped roof, small ventilator and chimney. *1134/641*

**Yeovil (Town), Somerset.**
**Yeovil (Pen Mill), Somerset; both 16 August 1960.**
I record in the text on page 158 the enjoyable day that I spent at Yeovil, which subsequently produced an article for *Railway World*. It is another town, like Bicester (page 28), that has retained two stations, though the Town station featured here closed in 1966. What a multitude of items to look at! The signal box is the reason for it being in this section; it controls shunt signals, distinguished by the rings on their arms, as well as more conventional ones. Just look at all the point rodding in the centre of the view. Note also the engine shed in the right background.

At the time that I photographed the Town station it was still used by a service which originated at the station in the lower view, Pen Mill, and went forward to Langport and Taunton; it was withdrawn in 1964. On the left is a wooden-post signal supporting a 3-foot metal arm and 'theatre' indicator. In the right foreground the post is of tubular steel with 4-foot metal arms, motor-operated distant and white sighting boards. At the bottom of the picture, the middle track contains an ATC ramp and detonator placers. By the water column is a brazier in anticipation of freezing conditions, and the station lighting is by gas. Apart from the up train in the platform, there are at least three other freight trains awaiting paths! And what a variety of rolling-stock! *2170/2168*

***Above*** **Yeovil (wartime junction), Somerset; GWR 'County' 4-6-0 No 1008 *County of Cardigan*, 1.45 pm Weymouth-Westbury, 16 August 1960.**
***Left*** **Maiden Newton, Dorset; GWR '57XX' 0-6-0PT No 3746, 11.05 am from Bridport, with No 3737 in siding, 13 July 1957.**
I'm quite proud of the Yeovil picture. Clearly I must have devoted more time than usual to its composition. Every piece of the junction is visible and the locomotive has fitted perfectly between the signal posts. I will have used a tripod and walked up and down the top of the cutting until satisfied that I was in the optimum position.

At the next junction to the south, Maiden Newton, the stock of trains for Bridport was fly shunted between journeys, taking advantage of the down gradient into the bay. *2165/1042*

***Above right*** **Chipping Campden, Glos; GWR 'Castle' 4-6-0 No 7025 *Sudeley Castle*, 10.55 am Hereford-London (Paddington), 26 July 1963.**
***Right*** **Three Cocks Junction, Powys; LMS '2MT' 2-6-0 No 46509, 10.52 am Brecon-Builth Road (Low Level), 30 May 1962.**
Main line and branch junction. The box bearing the name 'Campden Signal Box' is referring actually to Chipping Campden, and the station used to be sited behind the camera. Nice old level crossing gates. I'm on my way to Newtown in Powys, which was readily accessible by train from Three Cocks Junction (see page 10). The shuttle service to Builth Road (Low Level) is standing behind the box. *2963/2657*

A 22

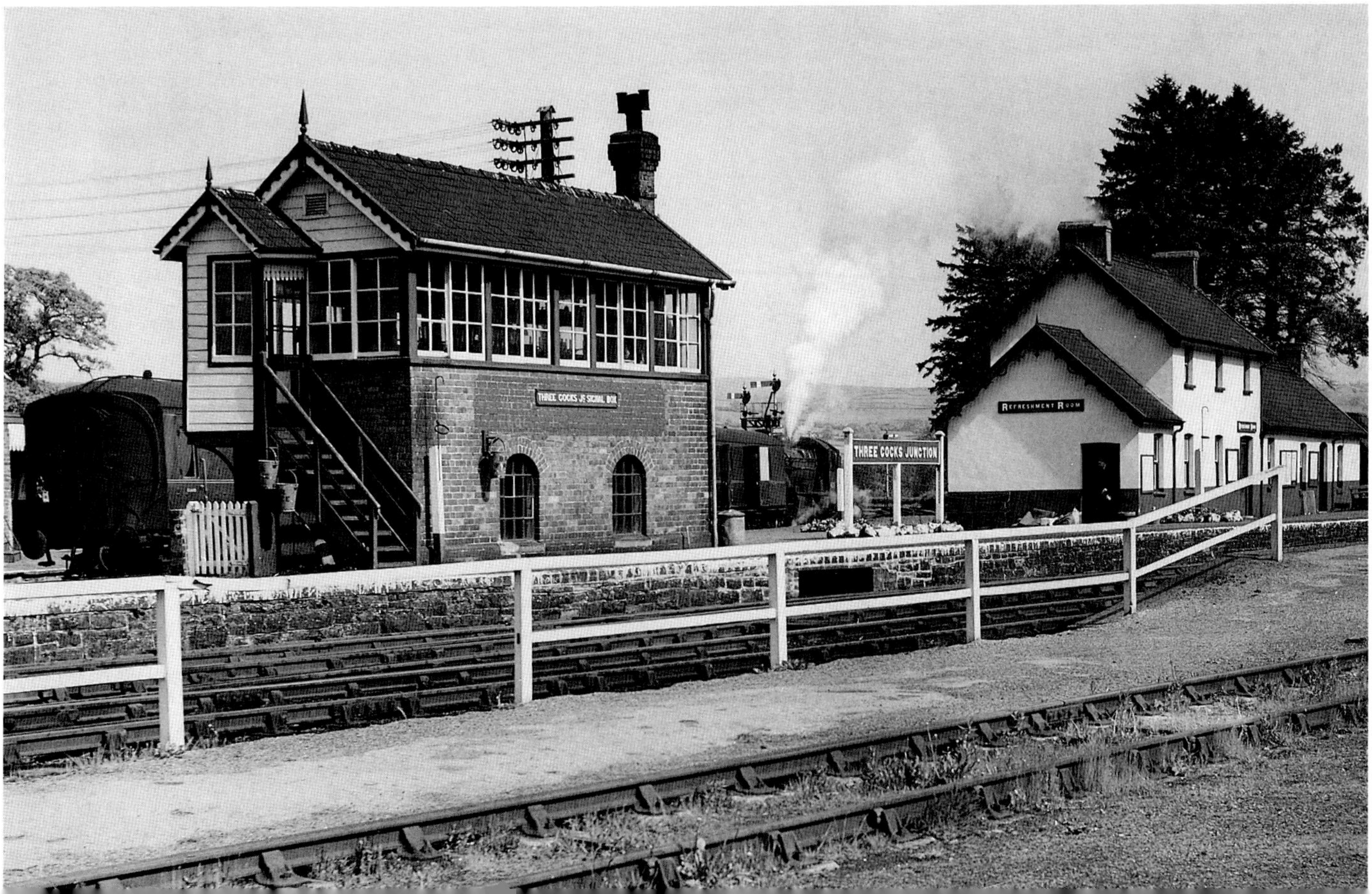
THREE COCKS Jn SIGNAL BOX
THREE COCKS JUNCTION
REFRESHMENT ROOM

Heriot, Borders; unidentified BR '4MT' 2-6-0, southbound light engine, 2 September 1965.
Shapwick, Somerset; LMS '2MT' 2-6-2T No 41243, 9.50 am Highbridge-Templecombe, 27 February 1965.

Two signal boxes that are many miles apart. The upper controls a crossing between Edinburgh and Hawick on the former Waverley route. The lower is sited by a loop between Highbridge and Glastonbury on the original Somerset & Dorset route. *3523/3360*

**Fenny Compton, Warks; WD '8F' 2-8-0 No 90701, South Wales-Woodford Halse freight, 24 July 1960.**
**Soudley No 1 Crossing Ground Frame, Glos; GWR '57XX' 0-6-0PT No 7723, empties to Bilson Colliery, 6 May 1958.**
Finally, two freight trains passing signalling facilities. First a wartime box on the GWR between Banbury and Leamington where connection was made with the Stratford upon Avon & Midland Junction line (now just to the military base at Kineton). The train appears to be creeping round the back, but in fact is on the through west-to-east route.

The installation at Soudley is a ground frame, sited where the branch from Bullo Pill on the Gloucester/Chepstow route emerges from the tunnel. *2131/1242*

# 16. London commuter lines

The photograph at New Malden (opposite) is one of the most significant in my collection from a personal point of view. I had always wanted to meet Bob Kirkland, a respected railway historian, and I knew Phyl, his wife, from County Hall, but had never had the courage to ask her if I might be introduced. Here they stood on the platform with the same aim in mind as myself - to photograph an up train on the down line. A valued friendship resulted and also the beginning of my academic education in transport which led in due time to a Diploma in Transport Studies and an MSc degree, followed by the professional qualification of a Fellowship in the Chartered Institute of Transport and a place on their Council.

At Kingston (also opposite) the engineer's train is rostered in connection with the replacement of the bridge over Richmond Road. When the extension to New Malden was mooted in the late 1860s a level crossing was envisaged at this point - imagine the congestion that this would have caused. In the event a low bridge was provided with a deep slope in the highway down and up. This used to flood at times of heavy rain and the trolleybuses were reluctant to pass through. Rebuilding has subsequently led to one-way traffic flow as part of an inner ring road.

On the day of the photo at Ashurst (page 169) I was taking local government examinations in London. By about three o'clock I had got fed up with the paper, hoped I had written enough, and set off for home and the car. The train used to divide at Ashurst, one portion going ahead to Lewes and Brighton, the other being taken by the loco in the yard, whence it returned to Tunbridge Wells West. At a country station like Melton Mowbray (page 124) it was quite a novel moment, but here it happened regularly and there was a member of staff familiar with uncoupling coaches. I travelled from Lewes on the up working one day and we were shunted into the up siding at Ashurst to listen to the birds singing until the branch coaches arrived and were attached. This time our engine stayed behind. Incidently, I did pass the exam!

The goods at Banstead (page 168) reminds me of Roy Mewett who used to live nearby. He was the Personnel Officer at the Local Authority Association to which I was appointed towards the end of 1967. I had planned to drive Ian to Plymouth later on the day of my interview to see two steam locos and preserved rolling-stock being taken up the Great Western main line next morning. This was a very unusual event at that time and was not to be missed. As I got the job it was natural that the Secretary should want to see me later. How to get to Plymouth with the car? Thus almost my first words to Roy were to enquire if I might use the phone. I rang Paddington and asked whether at this late stage it was still possible to take two passengers and the car on the Motorail to Plymouth that night. Someone there was happy to oblige.

When we eventually arrived at Paddington we were asked to drive across 'The Lawn', up a ramp over the buffers and through a line of covered vans, slowing at the ramp between each one. I needn't have worried about overcrowding - we were almost the only ones travelling. And 1st Class too, of course, in the light of the day's events! What a good way to start a new career (although it rained almost all the next day).

I could hardly have known when I took the picture from the Cromwell Road bridge (page 169) that it would be the route by which European trains through the Channel Tunnel would come to their maintenance depot. This line, the West London and West London Extension, has always had an interesting service over the years and the future will be no exception.

Widford Station (page 171) is of interest to me. At one of the many crises in the provision of rural transport, I took part in a TV item in the evening news on BBC talking about how local authorities might help finance some bus services. This was filmed at Forest Green in Surrey and I was asked if I could recommend a rural station in the outer London area where the train service had already been lost and the buses might follow. The result was a clip of a derelict Widford. There is little doubt in my mind that had the Buntingford branch been electrified and had the planning authorities been willing to have some suitable housing development, then the branch would be running today. It closed to passengers in 1964.

**Kingston, Greater London; LSWR '700' 0-6-0 No 30692, engineer's train, 23 March 1958.**

**New Malden, Greater London; SR 'West Country' No 34046 *Braunton*, 8.14 am Weymouth-London (Waterloo), diverted to down main line, 4 October 1959.**

The first railway reached Kingston-upon-Thames from Twickenham in 1863; the loop line as we know it was completed to New Malden in 1869. The engineer's train is standing on the line put in at that time to provide two new tracks, parallel with the existing main line on the north side at New Malden. Hence the up express in the lower picture, running the wrong way as it were, has just entered the original up line from Kingston, which comes into view from the left at about the third coach. The 'C' board on the platform marks the commencement of the speed restriction; the 'feathers' above the colour lights are route indicators for crossovers and for divergence to Kingston. *1201/1842*

30692
30692
83
PERRING
ON PAID UP
SHARES
ON INCENTIVE
SHARES

NEW MALDEN
383
8
C
C

**Banstead, Surrey; SR 'N' 2-6-0 No 31832, shunting, 24 May 1963.**
**St Helier, Greater London; BR '4MT' 2-6-0 No 76030, coal from Wimbledon, 13 March 1963.**
Two photographs of freight on commuter lines. Banstead is sited on the branch from Sutton to Epsom Downs, which is single track only now south of Belmont, and most of the extensive sidings and yard at the terminus have become housing estates.

The former London County Council built an extensive housing estate at St Helier which the London Underground expected to serve. Not so. The Southern Railway stepped in and held the District at bay in Wimbledon. The new line was built to gradients more suitable for electric traction than steam and few locomotives went south of here, where a small goods yard was provided. *2886/2041*

**Ashurst, Kent; BR '4MT' 2-6-4T No 80040, 4.49 pm London (Victoria)-Brighton via Lewes, and SR 'Q' 0-6-0 No 30549, waiting to take portion of train to Tunbridge Wells (West), 7 June 1962.**
Stockbroker-belt commuters now use a route cut back at Uckfield and without its link to Tunbridge Wells. I have never understood why this had to be closed - it could easily have been enclosed in a tunnel through Sainsbury's and would have brought even more shoppers to their doors. Do note the loading gauge on the right. *3044*

**Lillie Bridge, Greater London; LMS '2MT' 2-6-2T No 41292, Clapham Junction-Kensington (Olympia) ECS, 3 August 1960.**
To the left to Willesden, to the upper right to Clapham Junction and right downstairs to Earl's Court (with junction from Richmond & Ealing Broadway). The train is coming to take Post Office Savings Bank workers to their homes after work. *2143*

**Near Moor Park, Herts; BR '4MT' 2-6-4T No 80141, 2.52 pm Brackley (Central)-London (Marylebone), 29 August 1959.**
**Aylesbury (Town), Bucks; LMS '4MT' 2-6-4T No 42283, 3.00 pm from London (Baker Street), 20 September 1959.**
The direct line between London and Aylesbury has always been distinctive. Special regulations governed fares and ticketing and piles of books of these were on the waiting room table at Whitchurch Town on 19 February 1959 for some unknown reason. Built by the Metropolitan, their trains from Baker Street used it through Aylesbury to Quainton Road and Verney Junction (see page 183). Then for more than half a century some of the Great Central expresses came this way from Marylebone to the North. For years motive power changed from electric to steam at Rickmansworth. When the first DMUs were introduced the Lord Chief Justice lived near Great Missenden and succeeded in persuading BR to provide 1st Class accommodation. Now, as you can see from the track, electric tube trains run as far as Amersham (though this is outside the former GLC area and is in Buckinghamshire), and BR run beyond there just to Aylesbury. The upper picture was taken prior to quadrupling the track; work is just starting on the left.

There is a mass of detail in the lower view of Aylesbury station. Bell tower, water column and container for the bag, signal, bicycle, platform trolley, people. *1815/1837*

**Widford, Herts; LNER 'N7' 0-6-2T No 69633, 11.50 am St Margarets-Buntingford, 11 October 1958.**
**Buntingford, Herts; LNER 'N7' 0-6-2T No 69688, 1.27 pm to St Margarets, 10 January 1959.**
A commuter line that closed down (16 November 1964 for passengers), the branch from St Margarets near Ware in Hertfordshire to Buntingford. This area has remained quite rural as a result and houses here are much sought after by up-market commuters. Widford might be in deep country if the photo is to be believed; the access looks like a drive into a park. At Buntingford station staff are having a word with the driver while a lorry is being loaded from the warehouse on the left. *1433/1476*

# 17. Railwaymen

My first four illustrations show signalmen engaged in handling tokens for the safe occupation of single-line sections by the trains in question.

If you take the unclassified road westwards from the A423 at Sandpit Farm between Marton and Long Itchington in Warwickshire, pass over the River Itchen and up the hill beyond you will find an insignificant footpath heading north. I haven't been there for years, so the situation may have changed, but if not you will ultimately come upon a huge girder bridge across a cutting once occupied by the line from Leamington to Rugby. It is of immense size, especially in relation to the footpath it carries, and of considerable height. Why it was built to such dimensions is still a mystery to me. From it, towards Rugby, you could look down upon Marton Junction (see the frontispiece illustration on page 6) with the branch from Daventry and Weedon; we discussed its service earlier (page 68). After all the passenger services were withdrawn, cement traffic continued for some time between Long Itchington and Rugby, involving reversal beneath the bridge.

We have discussed the activities of the staff on the Coniston branch freight (page 92); at Torver (page 177) some of them seem to be inspecting the wild roses.

Trawsfynydd station (page 177) closed in 1961 with the line from Bala, which was partly submerged in a reservoir. Trawsfynydd Lake Halt had closed a year earlier, but came to life again as a terminal when the nuclear power station was commissioned. For years it had been suggested that the Great Western and LMS branches to Blaenau Ffestiniog should be connected to assist tourist traffic, but it was never done. Then, in order to handle nuclear fuel, the line north of the new terminal was reinstated and the missing link provided at last so that this could continue to Llandudno Junction. When Trevor Owen and I witnessed the movement of the nuclear flask on 19 April 1989 the train was being propelled the seven miles south from Blaenau Ffestiniog and the Guard was looking ahead leaning on the back of the brake-van smoking a pipe. How very British! Although it only ran on a Wednesday the local permanent way gang decided that this was the time to set light to the lineside undergrowth near Bont-Newydd. They arrived during the layover at Trawsfynydd and their fires held up the returning train for quite some time. Helpful for getting more pictures of the train.

At Gilling (page 179) the Guard of the freight train asked me to photograph him, the driver and fireman, and this was duly done at the convergence of the Malton and Helmsley lines. Someone borrowed the negative and I have not seen it for years. Then at Pockley Crossing the driver - Ernest Tong - had to open the gates and it was my turn for a picture (page 179). This appeared on the front cover of *The Railway Magazine* in April 1961, and had a sad sequel in that Mr Tong had subsequently died and his widow wrote to say that seeing his picture on a bookstall had given her rather a shock. Later on the journey he was to be very kind to me in locating the train precisely for a picture on Kirkdale Viaduct. The crew had arranged for Alan and myself to join them in coffee and cakes on the platform at the closed station at Nunnington while the loco steamed quietly with its line of wagons. The station is now a first class restaurant known as Ryedale Lodge.

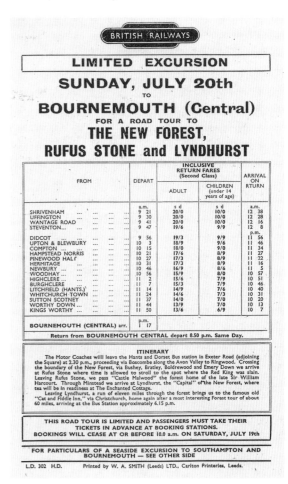

BRITISH RAILWAYS

**LIMITED EXCURSION**

**SUNDAY, JULY 20th**

TO

**BOURNEMOUTH (Central)**

FOR A ROAD TOUR TO

**THE NEW FOREST, RUFUS STONE and LYNDHURST**

| FROM | DEPART | INCLUSIVE RETURN FARES (Second Class) | | ARRIVAL ON RTURN |
|---|---|---|---|---|
| | | ADULT | CHILDREN (under 14 years of age) | |
| | a.m. | s d | s d | a.m. |
| SHRIVENHAM ... ... ... ... | 9 21 | 20/0 | 10/0 | 12 38 |
| UFFINGTON ... ... ... ... | 9 30 | 20/0 | 10/0 | 12 28 |
| WANTAGE ROAD ... ... ... | 9 41 | 20/0 | 10/0 | 12 16 |
| STEVENTON... ... ... ... ... | 9 47 | 19/6 | 9/9 | 12 8 |
| | | | | p.m. |
| DIDCOT ... ... ... ... ... | 9 56 | 19/3 | 9/9 | 11 56 |
| UPTON & BLEWBURY ... ... ... | 10 3 | 18/9 | 9/6 | 11 46 |
| COMPTON ... ... ... ... ... | 10 15 | 18/0 | 9/0 | 11 34 |
| HAMPSTEAD NORRIS ... ... ... | 10 21 | 17/6 | 8/9 | 11 27 |
| PINEWOOD HALT ... ... ... | 10 27 | 17/3 | 8/9 | 11 22 |
| HERMITAGE ... ... ... ... | 10 31 | 17/3 | 8/9 | 11 16 |
| NEWBURY ... ... ... ... ... | 10 46 | 16/9 | 8/6 | 11 5 |
| WOODHAY ... ... ... ... ... | 10 56 | 15/9 | 8/0 | 10 57 |
| HIGHCLERE ... ... ... ... ... | 11 2 | 15/6 | 7/9 | 10 51 |
| BURGHCLERE ... ... ... ... | 11 7 | 15/3 | 7/9 | 10 46 |
| LITCHFIELD (HANTS.) ... ... ... | 11 14 | 14/9 | 7/6 | 10 40 |
| WHITCHURCH TOWN ... ... ... | 11 24 | 14/6 | 7/3 | 10 31 |
| SUTTON SCOTNEY ... ... ... | 11 37 | 14/0 | 7/0 | 10 20 |
| WORTHY DOWN ... ... ... ... | 11 44 | 13/9 | 7/0 | 10 13 |
| KINGS WORTHY ... ... ... ... | 11 50 | 13/6 | 6/9 | 10 7 |
| BOURNEMOUTH (CENTRAL) arr. | p.m. 1 17 | | | |

**Return from BOURNEMOUTH CENTRAL depart 8.50 p.m. Same Day.**

**ITINERARY**

The Motor Coaches willl leave the Hants and Dorset Bus station in Exeter Road (adjoining the Square) at 2.30 p.m., proceeding via Boscombe along the Avon Valley to Ringwood. Crossing the boundary of the New Forest, via Bushey, Bratley, Boldrewood and Emery Down we arrive at Rufus Stone where time is allowed to stroll to the spot where the Red King was slain. Leaving Rufus Stone, we pass "Castle Malwood" the forest home of the late Sir William Harcourt. Through Minstead we arrive at Lyndhurst, the "Capital" of the New Forest, where tea will be in readiness at The Enchanted Cottage.

Leaving Lyndhurst, a run of eleven miles through the forest brings us to the famous old "Cat and Fiddle Inn," via Christchurch, home again after a most interesting Forest tour of about 60 miles, arriving at the Bus Station approximately 6.15 p.m.

**THIS ROAD TOUR IS LIMITED AND PASSENGERS MUST TAKE THEIR TICKETS IN ADVANCE AT BOOKING STATIONS.
BOOKINGS WILL CEASE AT OR BEFORE 10.0 a.m. ON SATURDAY, JULY 19th**

**FOR PARTICULARS OF A SEASIDE EXCURSION TO SOUTHAMPTON AND BOURNEMOUTH — SEE OTHER SIDE**

L.D. 302 H.D. Printed by W. A. SMITH (Leeds) LTD., Carlton Printeries, Leeds.

**Near Winchester Junction, Hants; GWR '43XX' 2-6-0 No 6343, Swindon Works outing to Bournemouth via DN&SR, 20 July 1958.**
Railwaymen and their families en mass! This is a Swindon Works outing to the coast. According to the 1-inch OS map Alan Wilson and I are at Woodham Farm; it was a long walk to get here and a bull took a dislike to his dog, Bustamente, so that we had a hasty departure! In an adjacent cutting to the right is the main line from Waterloo to Southampton, and a wartime connection to this, at Winchester Junction with the Alton line, is on the right horizon. The Didcot, Newbury & Southampton was normally shut on Sundays, so to run this train signalmen had had to come on duty in the morning at Enborne Junction and all the loops to the south and return to their posts again in the evening. Fantastic! Such expense would never be allowed today. *1364*

6343

**Blencow, Cumbria; LMS '2MT' 2-6-0 No 46491, Manchester (Exchange)-Keswick holiday train, 21 August 1965.**
**Crossmichael, Dumfries & Galloway; LMS '5MT' 2-6-0 No 42908, freight to Stranraer, 22 July 1963.**
Tablet exchanges on single lines: from Penrith to Blencow and from there to Penruddock in the upper view; from Castle Douglas to Crossmichael and from there to New Galloway in the lower. At Blencow the driver has thrown the staff on to the platform, whereas Crossmichael illustrates a real textbook exchange with both tablets caught perfectly. Here you could be mistaken in thinking that Diaghilev has choreographed the action. *3495/2951*

**Amlwch, Gwynedd; unidentified LMS '2MT' 2-6-2T, 2.25 pm to Bangor, 24 May 1962.**
The Guard looks really relaxed in the sun, waiting time to return to Gaerwen and Bangor. Someone's tried to keep the station nice with a few flowers, but it closed in 1964. *2637*

**Llanbrynmair, Powys; GWR '43XX' 2-6-0 No 6378, 9.55 am Aberystwyth-Shrewsbury, 22 August 1959.**
Slight apprehension about the signalman here as he waits to exchange tokens. Look how the point rodding disappears under the platform and into the box. The arm below the signal ahead has always puzzled me; it looks only half there! *1800*

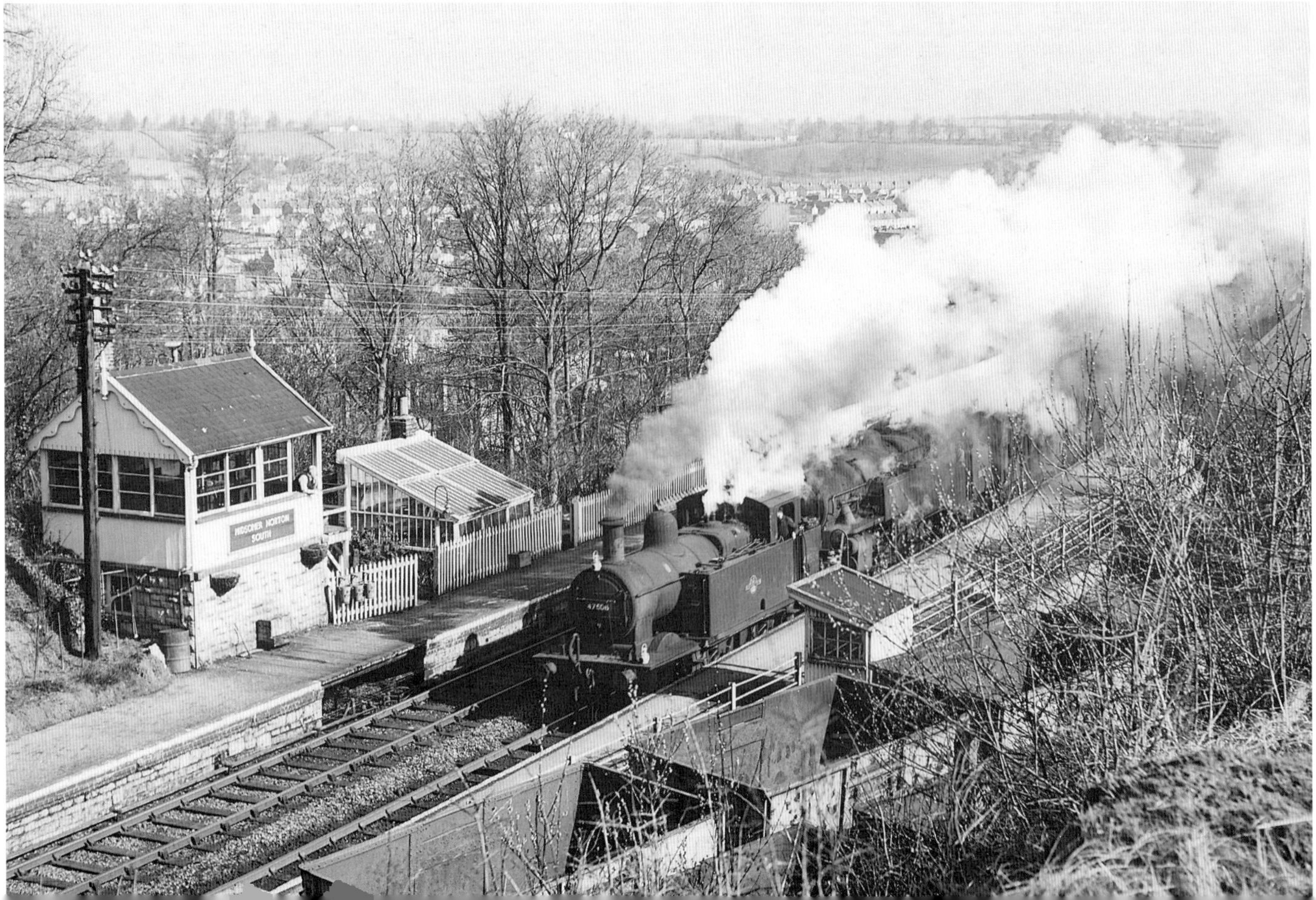
MIDSOMER NORTON
SOUTH

*Left* Redgate Mill Junction, Sussex; SECR 'L' 4-4-0 No 31773, 9.22 am Brighton-Tonbridge, 15 October 1955.
*Below left* Midsomer Norton South, Avon; LMS '3F' 0-6-0T No 47506 and BR '4MT' 2-6-4T No 80137, 9.05 am Bristol (Temple Meads)-Bournemouth (West), 26 March 1965.
We're on double track this time, so the signalmen are just having a look from their windows to see that all is well. At Redgate Mill Junction, where the 'Cuckoo' line to Hailsham and Eastbourne diverges to the left from the Lewes/Oxted line, he is worried about my safety, although I do have a track permit.

All is not well on the S&DR, however, where a shunting engine from the colliery working has had to be sent north to assist an ailing train. *647/3379*

*Right* Torver, Cumbria; LMS '3F' 0-6-0T No 47317, Barrow-in-Furness-Coniston freight, 1 June 1960.
What the staff are doing I really don't know. Even Harry was curious (see the text on page 92). Perhaps they are looking for cuttings for their gardens. *2027*

*Below* Trawsfynydd, Gwynedd; GWR '74XX' 0-6-0PT No 7414, 9.35 am Bala-Blaenau Ffestiniog freight, 12 May 1958.
Taking water at Trawsfynydd was obviously a social occasion - and perhaps a sad one in some ways. The old men, from the slate quarries perhaps, look as though they are recalling the days when they could be more active. I wonder how many gallons of water had been dispensed to locos from that column? *1280*

**Ashdon Halt, Essex; LNER 'N7' 0-6-2T No 69651, 4.06 pm Bartlow-Audley End, 22 March 1958.**
**Glemsford, Suffolk; LNER 'B17' 4-6-0 No 61666 *Nottingham Forest*, 2.43 pm Colchester-Cambridge, 27 June 1959.**
Gerald Daniels, Edwin Wilmshurst and I have come on from Takeley (page 108) and are pleased to photograph this vintage scene before it disappears. The station shelter is an old coach body, probably from the Great Eastern, and the driver is hunched over the controls in the driving trailer which is being propelled by the loco behind. Long macintoshes are in evidence on this cold March afternoon.

Staff one, customer one, at nearby Glemsford on the Stour Valley Line. Note the hand crane in the yard. Unless the porter does something about it, there will be no lighting tonight; perhaps he is in the process of refilling the oil lamp. *1196/1719*

**Gilling, North Yorks; LNER 'J39' 0-6-0 No 64928, 8.50 am Malton-Kirkbymoorside freight. Pockley Crossing, North Yorks; same train, both 26 May 1960.**

On my present doorstep: the Gilling picture has even appeared in the newly published Ryedale Guide. The signalman has come out to collect the token from Malton and to hand over the one for Kirkbymoorside; someone appears to have a parcel for Driver Tong.

Because of the absence of staff he had to open the gates himself for the train at Pockley (about a mile from my present home), while the fireman looked after the engine. The sad sequel is recorded in the text on page 172. *1977/1982*

# 18. Enthusiast connections

I have divided this last section broadly into two parts. The first illustrates trains specifically chartered for enthusiasts, while the latter draws on pictures in BR days of lines that are now part of the preservation movement.

It is only real eccentrics who are prepared to travel along lines in open wagons, and these were used only when passenger stock is no longer allowed. Such a case was the former Kelvedon & Tollesbury Light Railway in Essex. Never a financial bonanza, it was on its last legs when the REC chartered wagons to run from Witham along the Great Eastern main line and then down the branch as far as Tiptree (picture at Inworth opposite). I was surprised to find that the firemen of the engine had been with me in the RAF during national service.

The RCTS chartered the much longer train seen loading at Whittlesea (also opposite). A picture in the local press the following week (seen in the Introduction on page 9) bore the caption 'Slave trade at Whittlesea' and showed Harry, Alan and myself together with John Edgington. Later the same day we travelled alongside the streets of Wisbech and Upwell on the tramway, and the heavens opened. What the good residents of adjacent houses, obviously enjoying their Sunday dinners, must have thought of these mad foreigners standing in wet straw under their umbrellas belies belief. I can still remember the scent of damp clothing that pervaded the main-line train back to King's Cross.

The picture of Challow (page 184) brings to mind Gerard Fiennes's attempts as General Manager to revise the outer suburban services into Paddington. 'A recent study in 1963,' he wrote in *I Tried to Run a Railway* (Ian Allan, 1967), 'had shown it to be losing over half a million pounds a year. It was slow, not very punctual; too many trains called at too many stations. The old boy network operated to such a degree that the Fishguard boat train called at Challow to pick up commuters.'

The RCTS was also responsible for the charter of the special being run round at Verney Junction (page 183). The restaurant-car in the photo gives me the opportunity to expand on an aspect of our UK journeys so far only touched on. It was Harry who introduced me to the joy of taking meals on trains, an experience of which I never tire. Obviously there would be occasions when the timing of our itinerary, in as far as joining and leaving trains was concerned, could raise doubts as to the availability of lunch or dinner. In those circumstances it was my duty to write to the BR catering HQ to ensure that we would be suitably fed.

A Mr Portman-Dixon, Head of the Hotels & Catering Division, was as good to me (and perhaps just as patient) as Cyril Rider. May I give you just two examples of his help?

The three of us were to join the Bournemouth-Newcastle train one Saturday at Reading West at 1.52 pm, and alight from it at Rotherham Central at about 6.30. Too late for lunch and too early for dinner. So I wrote and explained our fears. I was assured that all would be well, and indeed it was! The restaurant-car steward was actually looking for us and recommended the steak and kidney pudding that was on the menu. He said that dinner would be served to us early on leaving Nottingham (Victoria). His only stipulation was that we should remain in the dining-car and always have a pot of tea on the table. This suited us very well. The train itself was to prove of interest. It left Reading West behind a Southern locomotive, changed to a Great Western engine at Oxford, a Stanier Class '5' at Banbury and a diesel at Nottingham. Because the 25 inches of vacuum had not been destroyed at Banbury, the brakes failed to release properly and we crawled up the hill out of the Cherwell valley towards Woodford Halse and never regained full speed until north of Nottingham.

The other catering incident for which we have space concerned the 1 pm Waterloo-West of England express. When the Western Region took over the operation of the route west of Salisbury it soon set about reducing its competitiveness with its own service from Paddington and withdrew the restaurant-cars. Harry, Alan and I were due to travel from Woking soon afterwards and I decided to write to Mr Portman-Dixon about late lunches as though no changes had taken place. To my surprise he replied that our request would be met. On entering the train we soon realised that catering was indeed limited to a buffet car, so I joined the queue to the counter. When I reached the attendant he cautioned me to be quiet but assured me that our lunches were there and that he would see to us as soon as the queue subsided. As good as his word, he then escorted us through the saloon, closed the sliding door behind us, and ushered us into a compartment where stood a table bearing a silver tureen full of fresh salad, plates laden with cooked ham, and appropriate cutlery, together with a cold sweet. He said that he must lock us in so that other potential customers didn't see us; he had advised them that lunch was not available. He would return after Salisbury with the coffee. And so we sat and enjoyed our lunch in private isolation, unable to see through the frosted glass window of a compartment that had been intended for a toilet, and slightly concerned about the lock in the hasp outside in the event of any accident to the train.

May I mention in conclusion two of the preserved railways. The Mid Hants (Alresford on page 189) brought my hobby and professional career together for the first time. I co-operated with the then Deputy Clerk of Winchester Rural District Council in seeking to avoid the closure from Alton to Winchester. While we failed, we now know from *British Railways 1948-73* by T. R. Gourvish (Cambridge University Press, 1986), commissioned by Sir Peter Parker when Chairman of BR, that the General Manager of the Southern had told BR HQ in June 1967 that he was unable to make an economic case for the closure', but had been over-ruled from there. F. C. Margetts is a name that must go down in history. I then became a Director of the company that preserved the line from Alton to Alresford, and gave up only in recent years.

It's appropriate that my last illustration (page 190) is of the Kent & East Sussex. Before meeting Hugh in Manchester, and just prior to my National Service, I had put my toe in the railway water in May 1951 and made my first journey over this line. I joined the 11.15 am from Charing Cross, which reached Headcorn in time to catch the 12.30 to Tenterden Town. This took 45 minutes to cover the eight miles involved, during which the hedgerows scraped the sides of the coaches and we stopped by request at High Halden Road, apparently for a chat, but not at Frittenden Road. I was fascinated by the sight of a tree seemingly growing horizontally from above the north portal of the short tunnel near St Michael's.

There was no ongoing train from Tenterden until 4.35, so I passed the time by riding to and from Rye on a bus. The train was then scheduled to take 55 minutes to cover the 13.5 miles to Robertsbridge, and it did. Shortly after leaving Rolvenden we stopped by a field gate; the guard then opened it and drove some pigs up planks that he had laid against the wagon that accompanied the one coach, and in which they travelled with me the rest of the way. I was very conscious of their presence on that hot May afternoon. The only other passenger joined at Junction Road Halt and alighted at Salehurst Halt.

This was the life for me. I hope you feel that the pictures do justice to some of our subsequent journeys, and that all my time has not been wasted!

**Inworth, Essex; GER 'J15' 0-6-0 No 65443, REC special from Witham, 6 April 1957.**
**Whittlesea, Cambs; GER 'J17' 0-6-0 No 65562, RCTS 'Fenman' special to Benwick, 9 September 1956.**
Most of what there is to say about these pictures is in the text opposite (and in the Introduction). The train at Inworth comprises two brake-vans and three fitted open wagons, while the RCTS charter started both in London and at Nottingham and the coaches, which met up at Peterborough, can be seen in the other platform at Whittlesea, where a somersault signal marks the right-hand horizon. I wonder what the lady is doing? 932/885

**Near Selham, Sussex; SR 'Q' 0-6-0 No 30549, 'West Sussex Downsman', London (Charing Cross)-Midhurst, 8 June 1958.**

**Bishops Waltham, Hants; LSWR 'M7' 0-4-4T No 30111, Branch Line Society special, 7 March 1959.**

Two specials on the Southern. Set 472 of Maunsell stock is being hauled along the branch from Pulborough to Midhurst by a Class 'Q' locomotive, which my adviser tells me was fitted with a BR Class '4' blastpipe and stovepipe chimney in August 1955. It will shortly pass above the road from Heyshott to South Ambersham along which I once travelled in a double-decker bus operated by Hants & Sussex Motor Services Ltd. It was on the 12 noon journey on Route 21 from Midhurst to Petworth, and as it approached the railway bridge great care was exercised to line up the vehicle so as to pass beneath in safety. I was in the front seat upstairs and I remember thinking that clearance was so tight that if the road was re-tarred a single-decker would be essential. It was, and a coach replaced the bus!

Bishops Waltham station and the branch from Botley lost its passenger service in 1933. This special, which was quite an event, had come from Lavant and was going to the Meon Valley. *1321/1527*

**Stanbridgeford, Beds; LMS '4F' 0-6-0 No 44414, 'The Cobbler' westbound, 19 September 1964.**
**Verney Junction, Bucks; LMS Class '5' 4-6-0 No 45091, RCTS 'Grafton Rail Tour' from Calvert to Banbury, 9 August 1959.**
East-west routes in the Home Counties north of London tended to have second-rate services and were closed before electrification could be carried out. One of the least-used lines ran from Leighton Buzzard to Dunstable on the London & Birmingham and from there through Luton to join the Great Northern at Welwyn Garden City. Connections at Dunstable were coincidence. So this special at the little-used wayside station of Stanbridgeford was a must for photography. The buildings look as though they haven't seen a paint-brush for a generation at least.

My favourite station, Verney Junction, is named after the landowner as no other community existed. *3325/1768*

**Challow, Berks; GWR '1361' 0-6-0ST No 1365, REC special from Faringdon, 26 April 1959.**
**Wolverton, Bucks; LNWR 'Special Tank' 0-6-0ST Nos CD7 and unknown, LCGB special to Newport Pagnell, 28 June 1958.**
Saddle-tank specials. Challow was a wayside station on the Great Western main line between Didcot and Swindon, and I talk about it in the text on page 180. It closed in 1964.

The Wolverton Carriage Works shunters were brought out to take a special to Newport Pagnell and back. *1593/1346*

**Sproxton, Leics; 4 April 1959.**

**Cannock & Rugeley Colliery, Staffs; LB&SCR 'E1' 0-6-0T No 110 *Burgundy*, now No 9 *Cannock Wood*, shunting, 21 October 1960.**

I have no wish entirely to ignore the industrial scene because we sometimes included trips there in our itineraries. Hence these two pictures. Railways seemed to come and go quickly in the ironstone country of Leicestershire where the loco is standing outside the makeshift shed.

The loco at Cannock & Rugeley Colliery in Staffordshire has a claim to fame. It started life as London, Brighton & South Coast Railway Class 'E1' No 110 Burgundy, and was sold in 1927 as Southern Railway No B110. It is now restored on the East Somerset Railway. *1553/2285*

**Cranmore, Somerset; GWR '57XX' 0-6-0PT No 3677, 11.12 am Yatton-Witham, 21 February 1959.**
**Same location; GWR '57XX' 0-6-0PT No 3643, same train, 11 May 1963.**
Cranmore station begins our small section devoted to lines that have become havens for preservationists, and it is logical to illustrate the East Somerset Railway first. The upper view shows a typical GWR brick signal box, and the lower bitumen wagons in the sidings. *1514/2874*

**Crowcombe, Somerset; GWR '4575' 2-6-2T No 5504, Minehead-Taunton freight.**
**Bishop's Lydeard, Somerset; GWR '4575' 2-6-2T No 5543, 1.40 pm Minehead-Taunton, both 26 February 1960.**
Not far away is the West Somerset Railway based on Minehead. I like visiting Crowcombe station because it is somewhat remote and very wooded. Bishop's Lydeard is presently the southern terminal, but doubtless Taunton will be reached regularly some day. Near Stogumber we suffered a puncture in a tyre of Geoff's car, so there are more memories here than of trains! *1880/1879*

IRON-BRIDGE
AND BROSELEY

61276

***Left*** **Iron Bridge & Broseley, Shropshire; unidentified BR '4MT' 2-6-4T, 11.35 am Bridgnorth-Shrewsbury, 27 October 1962.**
Although the Severn Valley Railway now terminates at Bridgnorth, it seemed a pity not to include this picture at Ironbridge, now tourist dominated but then very run down, so here it is. It is Saturday afternoon and, as at Newport at the beginning of our book (page 11), the ladies are going shopping - in Shrewsbury this time. Just look at the state of the station nameboard. *2767*

***Below left*** **Goathland, North Yorks; LNER 'B1' 4-6-0 No 61276, Whitby-Malton, 2 May 1964.**
Goathland has become even more famed through the recent TV series. Already the North York Moors Railway had brought tourists by the hundred - now these are augmented still further. Compared with today the sidings look quite forlorn. *3142*

***Right*** **Alresford, Hants; LSWR 'M7' 0-4-4T No 30029, 1.15 pm Eastleigh-Alton crossing the goods, 8 December 1956.**
***Below*** **Fletching Common, Sussex; LB&SCR 'C2X' 0-6-0 No 32442, 2.28 pm East Grinstead-Lewes, 7 August 1956.**
Two ex-Southern preserved lines. The origins of the 'Watercress Line', or Mid Hants Railway, are discussed in the text (page 180) - I was a Director for years. It's a busy scene at Alresford where the LSWR signal stands guard.

The lower picture was taken just south of the section now preserved as the Bluebell Railway. *908/860*

**Bodiam, Sussex; unidentified LB&SCR 'A1X' 0-6-0s, ramblers' special to Tenterden, 18 October 1959.**
And so to the last picture, on the unopened part of the Kent & East Sussex Railway between Northiam and Bodiam. Really this scene sums it all up for me - a quiet branch line in rich rural scenery on a sunny day. The castle just completes the view! *1844*

# Index of locations

**Postscript**
The perfect ending. The goods from Kirkbymoorside, hauled by LNER 'J39/2' No 64928, pauses at Nunnington. The Guard has arranged for the owners of Ryedale Lodge, who have taken over the station following closure, to provide the crew and us with coffee and cakes. After all, it is 11 o'clock in the morning! *Alan Lillywhite*